The Next Campaign: Bigger Ideas and Better Choices

John Michael Preston

ISBN-13:
978-1974397761

ISBN-10:
1974397769

This book is dedicated to my grandchildren's generation. I hope we can restore this country to a path that creates the best possible future for them. My grandchildren in descending order of age are Alexis, Grace, Isabella, Carter, Emilia, and Molly.

In 1961, President Kennedy joked that "Mothers all want their sons to grow up to be president, but they don't want them to become politicians in the process" (John F. Kennedy Quotes n.d.).

Special thanks to Jo Anne Simpson who insisted that I convert the talk I gave at the Unitarian Church of Charleston, following the 2016 election, into a book so that it would be accessible to more people.

I appreciate the input and feedback from my friends Fred Himmelein, Paul Forringer, and Bruce Gibb; my wife, Sally Preston; and my eldest son, Derek Preston.

John Michael Preston

About the Author

John is a retired professor who spends part of his retirement writing and making presentations on topics that interest him. He began his career as a high-school physics teacher, but after ten very successful years, he became restless and wanted to try his wings as an entrepreneur writing software for the new personal computers. He quit the best job in the school district, cashed in his retirement benefits, and started a software company named EnTech with his best friend, Bob Ferrett, that specialized in providing energy-consumption audits of small commercial buildings. A year later after a promising start, the government mandated that the public utilities provide this service for free.

Eastern Michigan University (EMU) was looking for someone with teaching, computer, and business experience to create a degree in energy management. John made the move and began a thirty-year career that included creating new degree programs in energy management and facility management. He was recognized by the International Facility Management Association as the outstanding educator of 1994. While at EMU, he coauthored more than sixty textbooks on using computer software with his friend Bob and his wife, Sally. He coauthored a book on project management and created two courses and wrote two textbooks for the basic studies requirement at EMU in quantitative reasoning and global awareness.

Since his retirement, he has delivered talks on nuclear power, the Iran deal, star power, monitoring your home over the Internet, and Vision for 2020—the inspiration for this book.

Contents

Foreword

In early November 2016, my wife and I were discussing our second oldest granddaughter and remarking on her talents and achievements during high school. She lives in the Deep South and has always been precocious. She was the first female to earn a place on the snare drum line in the high-school band. She works with special-needs children and has involved them in her dance recitals. The previous summer, students from a predominately black school were scheduled to be added to her high school, and there was concern about how the groups would interact. She took the initiative to reach out to students from the other school and propose that they meet, without teachers or adults, to discuss how to make these students feel welcome. She is a beautiful young woman, and her personality shines through on camera. She plans to be a communication major and attends Auburn University. I expressed my thoughts that I hoped she would become more than another television personality and that I thought she might make a good politician.

Because this was on the eve of what we thought would be the election of the first female president, I expected agreement from my wife. To my surprise, she said that politics is just too vicious and she wouldn't want her granddaughter to go through what it would take to get elected. I asked my stepdaughter if she would like her daughter to go into politics, and she had a similar response.

I pointed out to them that the two candidates for president had the lowest favorability ratings in forty years and that if we wanted to have better choices for public office, we needed to encourage our best and brightest children to run for office (Enten 2016).

I did a bit of research and found that a Gallup poll conducted in 2005 revealed that my wife and stepdaughter were representative of women in general. The poll showed that 67 percent of women did not want their child, of either gender, to become president (Carroll 2005).

The presidential election of 2016 did not result in the first female president, and it was conducted in a manner that supported my wife's opinion of the process. It did not surprise me to learn that 40 percent of those eligible did not prefer either candidate enough to vote (Harrington and Gould 2016).

I want to make our country the best possible place for my grandchildren to live in, and I'm sure that I share that goal with many others. I have not written this book for the money or the fame. My hope is to inspire some of our best people to run for office on a platform of new and better ideas that will encourage more people to vote and participate in the governance of our country to build a better future.

Chapter One
Create a Culture of Service and Higher Education

Thomas Jefferson—the primary author of the Declaration of Independence—was a strong supporter of free public education for all.

> *I know no safe depositary of the ultimate powers of the society but the people themselves; and if we think them not enlightened enough to exercise their control with a wholesome discretion, the remedy is not to take it from them, but to inform their discretion by education. This is the true corrective of abuses of constitutional power. Thomas Jefferson to William C. Jarvis, 1820 (Educating the People 1820)*

A committee, headed by Jefferson, drafted the Land Ordinance of 1785, which set aside one section (one square mile) of each county (thirty-six square miles) to fund public education that applied to five states: Michigan, Indiana, Wisconsin, Ohio, and Illinois.

> *Religion, morality, and knowledge being necessary to good government and the happiness of mankind, schools and the means of education shall forever be encouraged. (VanZant n.d.)*

I taught at Eastern Michigan University—a middle-tier university that provided affordable degrees for working-class people. I recall one afternoon when our president announced that we were now a state-assisted college rather than a state-supported college because the latest round of budget cuts had reduced the state's support to less than 50 percent of our costs. In the 1970s, state governments provided close to 75 percent of the cost of public college. By 2012, state support dropped to 23 percent (Douglas-Gabriel 2015). Prior to 1980, the federal Pell Grant program that is available to families that earn less than $30,000 a year paid for 77 percent of the cost of a public four-year college education. The program was cut significantly in the 1980s. By 2011, Pell Grants only pay for 36 percent. The difference in state support has translated into higher tuition and fees, which have been transferred into student loan debt. Two-thirds of students are graduating with debt. The average student debt is $37,000 (A Look at the Shocking Student Loan Debt Statistics for 2017 2017).

It can certainly be argued that colleges could reduce expenses, but the demonstrable effect of this reduction in funding is to increase tuition or add fees. If you have a child who is considering college, the prospect of paying for a college education is daunting. A four-year degree at a name university in another state will cost about $140,000, including tuition, fees, books, room, and board (Tuition Costs of Colleges and Universities 2014).

In this chapter, I propose some big ideas that tie college assistance to service while providing a better pool of political candidates and involving our youth in service to the country and the world.

Better Candidates: School of Diplomacy

I propose that we create a new academy that is like one of the military academies except that it is run by the State Department and is dedicated to producing diplomats. Students would receive this education at no cost in exchange for an eight-year service commitment. The upper-level classes would be taught by career diplomats, and students would study topics like trade, cultural exchange, negotiations, world religions and cultures, tourism, and national security. They would learn to play and appreciate international sports of the common people like football (soccer) and cricket and sports of the upper classes like golf, tennis, and racquetball. During summer internships and upon graduation, students would serve in US embassies around the world.

Following a successful twelve-year term of education and service, people in this program could qualify to return to school for three years to obtain a free law degree in exchange for an additional five years of service. The service would consist of three years working as a public defender or legal aid to the poor and two years as a congressional aide or aide to the Council of Economic and Financial Advisors (see #Council of Economic and Financial Advisors). As a congressional or council aide, they would put their legal education to work reviewing and drafting proposed legislation.

At the end of this twenty-year term, participants would be granted full retirement and health benefits. Because most of these people would be around forty years old, financially secure, experienced in international affairs, familiar with the problems of the poor, and the workings of Congress, they would form a pool of people who would have excellent qualifications to run for political office.

This plan would take decades to bear fruit, but the immediate benefit would be to provide an alternative path for our best and brightest who want to serve their country but who do not wish to do so in the military.

Disaster Response Corps
In the winter of 2005, there was a disastrous earthquake in Pakistan that killed more than 74,000, injured another 70,000, and left an estimated 2.8 million people homeless in October at the onset of winter (2005 Kashmir Earthquake 2009). It struck me that this was a golden opportunity for the United States to change the hearts and minds of Pakistanis and to lessen the influence of anti-Western militants.

The United States was one of many countries that responded. By March 2006, US aircraft flew five thousand sorties, delivered ten thousand tons of supplies, cleared forty thousand tons of debris, and treated thirty thousand patients. A study by the Pew Research Center in 2009 conducted a census of twenty-eight thousand households in the quake area and then randomly selected 10 percent of those households for detailed questioning. The results of the survey were clear:

Trust in foreigners increases to 60 percent as we move
to the immediate vicinity of the fault-line compared to

> *45 percent 20 kilometers away, and 30 percent 40 Kms*
> *away.*

The study concludes as follows:

> *We attribute the increase in foreign trust as we move*
> *closer to the fault-line to the increase in foreign aid and*
> *presence of aid workers. (Andrabi and Das 2010)*

Our military did a lot of good in response to this disaster, and the effect on the people of this region has persisted for at least four years. However, this isn't the mission the military is trained to do.

I propose that we create a Disaster Response Corp that is dedicated to helping other countries that have been hit hard by natural disasters such as earthquakes, volcanic eruptions, tsunamis, floods, and hurricanes. This corps would come in, help the people recover, and then leave. All without strings attached because that's what good neighbors do and it's who we are.

Young people who join the corps would receive training in the following skills:

- Operating and maintaining earth-moving equipment
- Establishing and maintaining emergency cell-phone systems
- Flying and maintaining helicopters
- Restoring sanitation and clean water systems
- Providing emergency medical assistance

The corps would use existing military transportation and relevant training facilities, which would provide additional funding for the military in these areas.

During their training, participants would study at a local community college or online to obtain a two-year associate's degree in their technical specialty. In exchange for the training and free tuition, participants would commit to six years of part-time service. For three years, participants would be on call to be deployed overseas. Employers would be required to hold the corps member's job and benefits while they are serving. Following their foreign service, participants would be on-call for three years to respond to disasters within the United States. While participants are on-call for six years, they would train one weekend a month to update their skills and maintain unit responsiveness.

After the training and overseas service periods, participants would have a two-year degree in a technical specialty, field experience, international travel, and good prospects for employment. Participants would receive a stock index fund (see Individual Stock Funds for Retirement), eligibility for support if they lose their job due to automation (see Automation Tax), and a minimum income guarantee (see Universal Income).

US Service Corps
In World War II, the military often brought people together from different backgrounds. An unintended consequence of this practice was that people got to meet, live with, and serve with people from other walks of life whom they would not have met otherwise and to form friendships and promote understanding (Colley 2003).

I propose that we create a US Service Corps that would expose our young people to each other from across the country while providing service to the country. The intent is to create awareness of the diversity of living environments, ethnicities, religions, and values that make up this country and to form personal relationships across those boundaries while providing support for other programs mentioned in this book.

The US Service Corps would be a full-time, two-year experience, intended primarily for young people who haven't started college or who have dropped out of high school. Units would consist of people from a variety of backgrounds, and participants would relocate every two or three months. Participants would perform unskilled or low-skilled service that is designed to expose them to a wide range of life in the United States, such as the following:

- Maintaining and building trails and infrastructure in national parks

- Helping veterans at VA hospitals
- Providing childcare for the working poor
- Going on ride-alongs with police officers to learn about law enforcement
- Monitoring video cameras in prisons to protect young inmates from hardened criminals
- Monitoring school hallways to improve school safety
- Helping with restorative-justice counseling in schools
- Serving in food preparation for the military and prisons

Corps members would begin their service with an orientation and training period of six weeks that would include vigorous outdoor labor such as building and maintaining trails in the national parks to improve their physical fitness.

Participants would spend part of each day studying online to earn a GED, a two-year associate's degree, or to take the basic studies courses that would transfer to a college of their choice.

In exchange for two years of service, participants would receive two years of college tuition, a stock index fund (see Individual Stock Funds for Retirement), eligibility for support if they lose their job due to automation (see Automation Tax), and a minimum income guarantee (see Universal Income).

Senior Service Corps

The church I attend has an annual budget of about a million dollars. Two years ago, there was a substantial budget shortfall, and the office manager left. Instead of hiring a replacement, one of the congregants volunteered to fill the position for a year. This man was a senior manager at an auto company before he retired. With the support of the congregation, he reorganized our existing debts, revised our procedures to make our books pass an audit and then used that improved financial statement to renegotiate our mortgage and reduce our monthly payment by more than a thousand dollars.

I retired a few years ago, and I was looking for something meaningful to do. Prior to teaching technology at the college level for thirty years, I taught physics at the high-school level, and my teaching certificate is still valid. I know that many high schools do not have teachers with degrees in physics to teach physics classes, so I considered teaching one or two hours a day to provide the local students with a better educational opportunity. I found out that the existing structure was not flexible enough to take advantage of my offer (see #Make Schools Smaller) (see #Use Retirees to Teach Part Time).

I propose that we create a Senior Service Corps to take advantage of the wealth of experience and expertise in the older segment of our population. It would match retired volunteers with jobs in nonprofits, schools, and churches.

Chapter Two

Improve Voter Participation and Civil Discourse

I vote in most elections, so I've been trying to understand why so many people do not vote. I am a white male with above average income, and I've never voted in an election where I was part of a minority that had no chance of electing someone who was at least superficially like me, so I can understand why people who are in a racial minority might not vote.

Another reason that occurs to me is that in districts where one party dominates, the real election is in the primary, and if the primary is limited to members of that party, the resulting candidate is sure of election with no input from me at all; so why vote?

It is also hard for anyone with new ideas to break into politics. Even though these candidates might attract a substantial percentage of votes, they are often more likely to appeal to supporters of one of the two leading candidates and are accused of being "spoilers," which forces us to vote for someone we don't really support to keep someone worse from getting elected. I really don't like holding my nose when I mark my ballot.

Finally, I am disgusted by the way elections can become trivialized and focus on personal character rather than on issues.

I suspect that these arguments occur to many of the people who comprise 40 percent of the eligible voters who do not want to stand in line on Tuesday night after working all day. The following ideas are offered to increase participation and improve the civility of the process.

Voter ID

I think that most of us can agree that we want to assure that the people who vote in an election are legally authorized to do so. Specifically, that they are citizens of the USA, of legal voting age, residents of the state or district in which they are voting, and that they only vote one time per election. While most voters have state driver's licenses that are generally accepted as a photo ID, the elderly who no longer drive and the poor who don't have cars do not.

In the presidential election of 2016, the winning candidate alleged that there was widespread voter fraud (Bradner 2017). I think the problem here is correctly placing the burden of proof on the person making the claim of fraud and making it easier for the accuser to make his or her case and punish the offender if the accuser is correct (see #Throw the Flag).

I propose creating a simple method of issuing a voter ID that has a picture; a biometric like a thumbprint, palm print, or retina image; and the voter's name, age, and address. The person operating the equipment would be a government official or would obtain a credential like a notary public. The person issuing the ID would attest that the picture and biometric are of the person before him or her, and he or she would also include his or her own name and biometric. The required equipment could be as simple as a smartphone with a photo printer and laminator. Because the equipment is cheap and portable, the ID could be obtained at senior centers and neighborhoods where fewer people own cars in addition to government offices. The applicant would fill out a form in which he or she affirms his or her status as a legal citizen with the date and city of his or her birth, birth date, and address. The applicant would also acknowledge that falsifying this statement regarding citizenship is grounds for deportation and making false statements on the form is punishable by substantial fines. The ID and its biometrics would be uploaded into a central voter database.

At the polling site, voters would have their photo ID scanned and recorded in a database. Each swipe of the voter ID at the polling place would be checked against a database to assure that the person had not voted more than once and that he or she was eligible to vote in that district. If someone alleges voter fraud, he or she would go to a judge and show cause for why he or she thought this might have happened. If the person had enough evidence to raise doubt about an election, the judge would make the appropriate databases available to a public prosecutor who would check to see if the allegation is true and then take steps to punish the person for making false statements, voting in the wrong district, or voting more than once. If there were evidence that the fraud was coordinated by someone or a political party, the prosecutor could widen the investigation beginning with the person issuing the IDs. If the person issuing IDs were cheating, his or her thumbprint on the fake IDs would make it easy to convict him or her.

The intent of this proposal is to make it easy to get a photo ID and place the burden of proof of voter fraud on the person making the allegation. If the fraud exists, prosecution would be aided by signed statements acknowledging responsibility and by public records of voting. This ID is not a certification by the state of the accuracy of its information, just that it was filled out by the person who matches the biometric information.

Weekend Elections

Some ideas are simple, popular, easy to implement, and have a high likelihood of improving our society but our system is too partisan to enact the ideas. An example is the proposal to change the day we vote for Congress and the President from the first Tuesday in November to the first full two-day weekend in November which would be more convenient for everyone. Consider the history of this idea in the U.S. Congress:

- 2005-06 109th Congress, Senate S.144, Voting from 6 pm Saturday to 6 pm Sunday, Referred to the Committee on Rules and Administration, not enacted (S.144 Weekend Voting Act 2005)
- 2007-08 110th Congress, Senate S.2638 and House H.R 6240. Neither enacted. Voting from 10am Saturday to 10pm Sunday, not enacted (S.2638 - Weekend Voting Act 2008)
- 2009-10 111th Congress, Senate S.149, H.R. 254; Voting from 10am Saturday to 6 pm Sunday, not enacted (S.149 Weekend Voting Act 2010)
- 2010-11 112th Congress, House H.R. 4183, Voting from 10am Saturday to 6 pm Sunday, not enacted (H.R 4183 - Weekend Voting Act 2012)

- 2011-12 113th Congress, House H.R. 1641, Voting from 10am Saturday to 6 pm Sunday, not enacted (H.R. 1641 - Weekend Voting Act 2014)
- 2012-13 114th Congress, House H.R. 3910, Voting from 10am Saturday to 6 pm Sunday, not enacted (H.R. 3910 - Weekend Voting Act 2016)
- 2013-14 115th Congress, H.R. 1094, Voting times left to states on Saturday and Sunday, not enacted, (H.R. 1094 - Weekend Voting Act 2018)

None of these bills ever got a vote in the House or Senate—they all died in committee. We need to fix congress by changing the way we elect people to the House of Representatives and begin making common-sense changes like this one.

Replace Winner-Take-All Elections

Article 1, section 2 of the US Constitution specifies that representatives be elected every two years and that the manner of their election is left to the states:

> *The Times, Places and Manner of holding Elections for Senators and Representatives, shall be prescribed in each State by the Legislature thereof; but the Congress may at any time by Law make or alter such Regulations, except as to the Places of chusing [sic] Senators.*

Section 2 also places an upper limit on the number of representatives:

> *The Number of Representatives shall not exceed one for every thirty Thousand, but each State shall have at Least one Representative; (U.S. Constitution n.d.)*

In 1929, Congress passed the Reapportionment Act of 1929 (Flores n.d.).

Every ten years, we have a census that tells us how many people there are and where they live. In the Fourteenth Amendment, section 2, the principle of proportional representation is repeated.

　　　　　　　　　　Replace Winner-Take-All Elections

We have 435 members of the US House of Representatives. Our population was 309 million in 2010, which is an average of about one congressperson per 710,000 residents (United States of America / Population (2010) 2010); (Members of Congress 2017). The states are allocated congressional seats based on population, so a state like South Carolina with a population of 4.6 million at the last census, has seven congresspersons.

The state legislatures redraw the boundaries of the congressional districts to reflect shifts in population. Each district elects one congressperson in a winner-take-all election. Due to the winner-take-all voting system and by carefully drawing the boundaries using a method called *gerrymandering*, more candidates from the party drawing the district lines get elected than are representative of the state as a whole. For example, Massachusetts has nine representatives, all of whom are Democrats even though about a third of the voters are Republicans (Massachusetts Registered Voter Enrollment: 1948-2016 2016). Similarly, about a third (34 percent) of Alabama voters are Democrats, but six of the seven congresspersons are Republicans.

The present method of electing people to the US House of Representatives uses a winner-take-all method where one candidate wins per district. The candidates are usually chosen by political parties in primary elections that precede the general election. In districts where one party is dominant, and the primaries are limited to members of that party, the outcome of the general election is already determined by the results of the primary election, and there isn't really a point in voting in the general election.

Another result of this system is that incumbents are almost unbeatable. For example, in California over a ten-year period from 2002 to 2012, only one seat changed parties out of 255 elections. The voters in California thought the problem was due to gerrymandering congressional districts (Nagourney 2012). In 2008, California voters passed a referendum named Voters First Act that gave the job of redistricting every ten years to a bipartisan and independent commission (Background on Commission 2014). The intent was to make more districts competitive, require candidates to appeal to minorities, and give new candidates a reasonable chance of winning or to change party control.

The California elections of 2012 used the newly drawn districts, but it did not work as well as hoped. The few contested elections occurred where two incumbents were placed in the same district. The conclusion drawn from this effort by a group named FairVote is that redistricting by itself does not make enough difference. The real problem is the winner-take-all method combined with single seat districts (Ranked Choice Voting 2017).

In addition to addressing gerrymandering, I propose a method of electing representatives to Congress that makes every vote count. In this method, congressional districts would be large enough to qualify for up to five seats in Congress. Instead of primaries, candidates would qualify to get their name on the ballot in each large district by gathering signatures or swipes (see #Voter ID) in that district—voters would be limited to signing or swiping for one candidate. For example, if Massachusetts qualifies for nine house seats, it would be divided into two election districts that would elect five and four representatives, and the number of candidates on the ballot in each large district would be ten and eight respectively. In the district that has five seats and ten candidates, the ten candidates with the most petition signatures would be on the ballot. The period allotted for gathering signatures would be six months.

To get elected in a district that will have four congresspersons, a candidate must have at least 25 percent (100 percent/seats) of the vote. When the votes are tallied, let's say that one candidate has more than 25 percent and is elected. The remaining three seats are built by coalition and deal making. The candidates with surplus votes choose how to distribute their extra votes, and those candidates with too few votes to be elected in the first round make deals with each other and the elected candidates until three of them reach the minimum to be elected.

Replace Winner-Take-All Elections

Here is a step-by-step example:

1. Divide the state into large districts that would elect three to five representatives.
2. The number of candidates would be twice the number of available seats (four seats, eight candidates).
3. Prospective candidates and their supporters circulate petitions. One petition signature is allowed per registered voter (see #Voter ID). The eight candidates with the most valid petition signatures are placed on the ballot. Using the new voter ID would greatly reduce the number of extra signatures required because they would be vetted as soon as they swiped a ballot registration.
4. Hold an election where each voter picks only one candidate out of the eight. The voting results in the following distribution:
    a. Candidate A: 30 percent
    b. Candidate B: 20 percent
    c. Candidate C: 15 percent
    d. Candidate D: 15 percent
    e. Candidate E: 8 percent
    f. Candidate F: 5 percent
    g. Candidate G: 4 percent
    h. Candidate H: 3 percent
5. Candidates with 25 percent or more of the vote are immediately elected to one of the four seats, so candidate A is elected immediately.
6. In the week following the election, the remaining candidates negotiate among themselves to achieve the necessary 25 percent. For example, candidate A could transfer the extra 5 percent of his or her total to candidate B for a promise of support, or candidate B might be willing to support candidate F's issue for his or her 5 percent.
7. After a week of negotiation, the four candidates with the highest net percentage are elected to the four seats.

In this system, everyone's vote counts. If you voted for a popular candidate, he/she might use your extra vote to make a deal for support from another candidate. If you voted for a candidate who didn't get enough votes to be elected initially, your vote still gives that person enough power to negotiate a deal to become elected or to at least extract a promise of collaboration from another candidate. If a candidate represents an extreme view like a neo-Nazi party that no one wants to associate with or if the candidate refuses to back anyone else, the candidate who is closest to the required percentage wins a seat.

In this example, if you are a member of a minority group of 15 or 20 percent, you can be confident that you will be represented if your candidate can make a deal with someone else. If you prefer the platform of a person who doesn't stand a chance of getting elected, instead of being a spoiler, you give your candidate the power to make a deal with another candidate to consider your point of view.

If a candidate might depend on the goodwill of an opponent to get elected, it should reduce the amount of negative attack ads during the campaign. There will still be backroom deals, but your candidate will have a seat at the table instead of the party elite choosing primary candidates who run unopposed. Unlike a parliamentary system, once the deals are made, the people who were not elected cannot take back their support. If someone shows that their word is no good, they will have trouble making deals in the next election that is only two years away. Outright bribery and selling of votes would be illegal.

Throw the Flag

When I was on the debate team in high school, we learned two important concepts. One was called *the burden of proof*, which is the obligation to prove one's assertions (Burden of Proof 2017). The other was that you cannot prove a negative. I've observed that our political discourse has become overwhelmed with unsupported assertions. Those who wish to challenge their accuracy are burdened with proving them wrong or proving a negative. It is far easier to tell

Throw the Flag

a lie than it is to prove it wrong, and those making the assertions can use electronic distribution and social media to overwhelm their opponents with sheer volume of untrue statements.

I was visiting a friend for dinner, and he had a neighbor at the meal who quoted Admiral Yamamoto of the Japanese navy as saying that Japan did not invade the mainland of the USA in World War II because "there would be a rifle behind every blade of grass." I didn't feel it was my place as a guest to challenge this statement, so I let it go because I didn't think I could prove that he never said something like that (there is no record of it) (Misquoting Ymamoto 2009).

In another instance, I was in the audience at a lecture on the health of the oceans and the person giving the lecture stated that sea level has been rising at a rate of one inch a year for the last several decades, and no one in an audience of two hundred (including me) challenged that assertion (it has risen eight inches since 1880, which is less than one-tenth inch per year and has increased to about one-eighth inch per year more recently) (Sea Level Rise 2017).

I checked these statements out later and confirmed that neither was correct. In a third conversation with my son-in-law, he stated that America had the highest corporate-tax rate among developed nations—it turned out he was right, but I was unduly skeptical of his following comments that were based on this assertion, which colored my openness to hearing what he had to say (Pomerleau and Potosky 2016). This taught me that there is a risk of being too skeptical of ideas that don't fit your present view. In this example, I should have challenged his statement at the time if only to validate it so I would consider his subsequent ideas more favorably.

Because many of my friends are sports fans, I propose that we adapt a sports metaphor to our political discussions. Before we participate in a political discussion, I suggest that we all agree that it is important to get the facts right. As Daniel Patrick Moynihan wrote to President Nixon:

> *Everyone is entitled to his own opinion, but not to his own facts. (Weisman 2010)*

We also must agree on what constitutes a reliable source. According to Reference.com, a reliable source is "any source that has competence in the field of interest, without any biases or conflicts of interest related to the topic" (What is the Definition of a Reliable Source? 2017). Examples of nonsources are Wikipedia, a "news" story that is merely repeating what a guest said, or single-author blogs with no editorial function to assure accuracy.

Once the ground rules are agreed upon, each of us gets to *throw the flag* if someone wants to challenge the accuracy of a statement. At that point, the conversation stops while the person making the statement either withdraws it or takes out his or her smartphone, iPad, or laptop and looks it up. Like a football game, each participant gets a limited number of challenges and loses one of them if the person who is challenged can verify his or her statement with a reliable source.

The intent of this proposal is to shift the burden of proof onto the person making the statement and make it clear to everyone in the discussion who is making unverifiable or incorrect statements. Losing a few of these challenges might discourage people from repeating rumors in the future, at least in conversations of which you are a part.

Truthfulness Ratings

One of the tactics I've observed in this last election cycle was how repetition was used to establish a falsehood in people's minds. Someone would make an outlandish claim, and the news media would report that he or she had said it. While it was true that the person said or tweeted the comment, the comment itself was false, but by repeating the statement, it becomes part of our memory and before long, it can be assumed to be true.

I propose that we establish a system of posting a visual rating of truthfulness that would appear on-screen prior to any political statement warning viewers if the speaker will say something that is without basis in fact, contradicts known facts, or is only partially true.

Websites like PolitiFact have a Truth-O-Meter that could be the basis for such a rating system (The Latest from PolitiFact 2017).

Tax-Return Voting

Unfortunately, only one in five of us has a good idea of how our federal tax money is spent (Bond 2014). If our spending reflects our values but we don't know where our government is spending our money, we have a disconnect between our spending and our values. I often hear people say they are fiscal conservatives but social liberals and that they have trouble choosing a candidate from either party. Fortunately, there is a way to

- focus attention on how our elected officials spend our tax dollars;
- indicate to Congress how we rank spending issues in importance to us;
- align our spending with our values; and
- give every taxpayer a voice in government spending.

I propose that we make a change to our annual tax returns that are filed electronically. There would be a section that shows a pie chart representing the president's proposed budget followed by a similar pie chart showing the opposition party's budget, like the one shown in Figure 1.

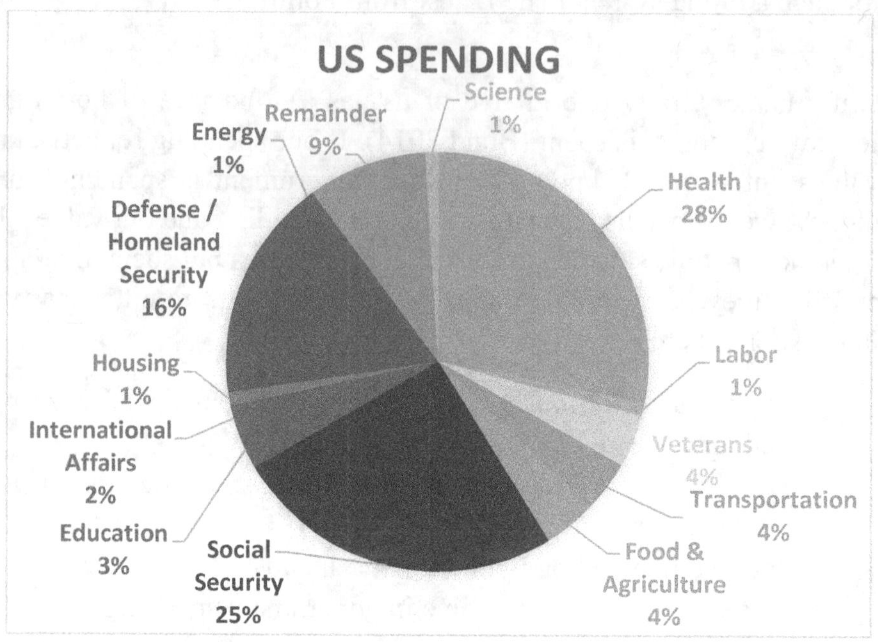

Figure 1

If a minority party like the Tea Party or the Green Party has 10 percent or more of the seats in the US House of Representatives, they could also propose a budget. Taxpayers could pick one of the proposed budgets. Each party would also propose five spending priorities that would be combined into a single list and then taxpayers would rank the spending priorities.

When the tax returns are filed electronically, computers would tally the "votes" for each budget and calculate the ranking of the spending priorities. The results would be reported to the public and the Congress.

Voters would also be able to indicate if they wanted congress to increase taxes to pay off the national debt (see <u>Balance the Budget</u>).

Chapter Three

License Small Militias

Our country is deadlocked in a struggle over gun safety. I see this as a symptom of mutual distrust between the opposing parties that characterizes discussions about topics like reproductive rights and gun ownership. Both sides assume that any reasonable compromise would be letting the camel's nose into the tent and the real agenda of the other side is an outright ban. I grew up owning and shooting a gun. My parents were from the rural south, and gun ownership was a part of life. When my father went off to school during the depression, my mother ran the country store they owned that included a small post office. She had to qualify as a postmaster in my father's absence, and at that time, she said that an applicant had to prove he or she owned and could fire a gun to get the job.

When I read the diary of Anne Frank in high school, I had a hard time identifying with her because I knew that if the Nazis came for me, I'd fight and be sure to take a few of them with me. It didn't occur to me that she couldn't get a gun with which to defend herself. I think it is important for gun-control advocates to realize that the government can become the enemy, and to prevent tyranny by the government like the Germans experienced, our founders put gun ownership in the Constitution as the Second Amendment.

I also observe that many gun owners only quote the second part of the Second Amendment. In its entirety, it is:

> *A well regulated militia, being necessary to the security*
> *of a free state, the right of the people to keep and bear*
> *arms, shall not be infringed.*

I propose that we apply the entire Second Amendment to this problem in a new way that might satisfy the needs of both sides of this issue.

Create Militia Licenses That Work like Liquor Licenses

We are familiar with licensing bars and restaurants to sell alcoholic beverages. Getting a liquor license is vital to the profitability of a restaurant or bar, and the owners are careful to avoid violating the rules for fear of losing their license. I propose that states license militias in a manner similar to the way they grant liquor licenses. All the state's licenses would require that all guns and ammunition be sold through a licensed militia to its own members. Membership would be limited to about two hundred, and there would be an annual membership fee.

Each new member must be sponsored by an existing member, and founding members would choose fellow members as sponsors. The militia's license owner and the member's sponsor would be responsible for vetting new members.

Protection of Gun-Ownership Rights

Some gun owners are deeply concerned about government confiscation of their guns, which is completely puzzling to nongun owners. Gun owners are opposed to registering their guns because they fear this would be the first step in confiscation. The militia, which is run by someone they know and trust, would keep a database of ballistic identification of each gun and who owns it. The ballistic characteristics of the guns would be searchable electronically by law-enforcement agencies. If the police had cause to think that a particular gun had been used in a crime, they would get a court order requiring the militia to identify the owner of the gun. Thus, the militia and the courts would serve as a buffer between government agencies and gun owners, preserving their privacy.

Responsibility for Gun Use

If a militia member is convicted of a crime or suicide involving a gun, the holder of the militia license would have to appear before the licensing body to show what he or she had done to prevent this person from using his or her gun illegally or to commit suicide (see #Graceful Exit). The militia license owner might lose his or her license if he or she had not demonstrated due diligence in vetting the member with background checks and responsiveness to changes in behavior. Similarly, the perpetrator's sponsor would have to explain what he or she did or did not do to prevent the crime. If the sponsor failed in his or her role, he or she could have his or her membership suspended or revoked depending on the severity or prior offenses. The idea is to make one's fellow militia members accountable for each other's behaviors with a substantial economic benefit or penalty.

Limitation of Manufacturing to Purchase Orders from Militias

One way to control the distribution of unregistered guns is to require gun manufacturers to make guns to order. The militia would place an order for its member, and the gun would be made and shipped directly to the militia for resale to its member.

Private Sale

Sales between individuals would be monitored by the militias to which the parties belonged. Sale of a gun by a militia member to a nonmember would be illegal and punishable by suspension of the person's militia membership and any fines imposed by the local militia or state licensing authority. Militia members would be required to periodically present their guns to the local militia to demonstrate that they have all the guns that are registered to them.

Concealed Carry and Confiscating Unlicensed Guns

A common argument is that if guns were illegal, only criminals would have guns. The challenge here is to identify who is carrying a gun and if he or she is a member in good standing of a licensed militia. Militia members would carry a membership card that indicated the name of their militia, their name, and date through which the card is valid and a chip like a credit card. Guns can be detected by scanners that can be built into doorways or into handheld wands. If a store or building owner wants to control access by gun owners to his or her building, he or she can install a detector with a card-reader stripe. Scanners and card swipe access points could be installed at schools, subways, and on buses. Similarly, police could check to see if someone was carrying a gun by running a wand over him or her. There is no need to frisk someone to tell if he or she is carrying a gun. If the police confirm that someone is carrying a concealed weapon and he or she doesn't have a valid militia membership, they could confiscate the gun and arrest the person. This method wouldn't eliminate unlicensed persons from carrying guns, but it would limit where they could take them and give the police a method of confiscating illegal guns.

     Concealed Carry and Confiscating Unlicensed Guns

Chapter Four

Take the Profit Out of Crime and Politics

When you try to put out a fire, you aim the fire extinguisher at the base of the fire where the fuel is rather than at the flame. The intent is to break the cycle of fuel, heat, vaporization, and flame. I like solutions to problems that disrupt the cycle so the symptoms die away from lack of sustenance. In this section, we look at taking the profit out of organized crime and political corruption.

A substantial fraction of our citizens finds pleasure, release, or forgetfulness in ways that a majority finds immoral. If that majority passes laws against that activity, we find our society at war with its own citizens. One cannot fight a war on drugs. Wars are fought against people. We learned a partial lesson in the 1920s when the country tried to prohibit the sale of alcohol. The result was funding gangs of criminals who used the money to buy guns and corrupt the police force (The Impact of Organized Crime in the City of Chicago n.d.). We need to apply that lesson to the situation today. The ideal solution would be to convince people that it is unhealthy to use drugs, but that approach is clearly not preventing the large-scale sale and distribution of drugs.

In a parallel development, our corporations have learned that it is easier to buy politicians than to abide by regulations or pay their share of taxes. In this chapter, we look at ways to take the profit away from organized crime and corruption of politicians so that the money is available for other programs described in this book.

Legalize Recreational and Addictive Drugs

Americans spend an estimated $109 billion a year on illegal drugs. That's an average of $336 a person for every man, woman, and child. The four principal drugs are marijuana ($41 billion), cocaine ($28 billion), heroin ($27 billion), and meth ($13 billion). In each of these categories, about 80 percent of the drugs are consumed by daily users (Kilmer 2014).

According to the National Institute on Drug Abuse, 4.2 million Americans are categorized as dependent or abusers of marijuana compared to 855,000 dependence/abuse of cocaine and 517,000 for heroin. The same report indicated there are 595,000 methamphetamine users without categorizing the percentage considered abusers (I'll assume 50 percent) (Nationwide Trends 2015). If we combine these three sets of statistics, we find that 6.1 million Americans are abusing or dependent on one of these four drugs, assuming minimum crossover between categories. The population of the country is 324 million, so this means that about 2 percent or one in fifty Americans has an illegal drug abuse or dependency problem. If we combine these statistics, we can estimate what daily drug use costs per person:

- 4.2 million daily users spend $32.8 billion (80 percent of $41 billion) a year on marijuana, or $7,809 each.
- 855,000 daily users spend $22.4 billion on cocaine or $26,200 each.
- 517,000 daily users spend $21.6 billion on heroin or $41,800 each.
- 297,500 (50 percent of 595,000) daily users spend $10.4 billion (80 percent of $13 billion) on meth or $35,000 each.

The cost for a daily user of heroin or meth is so high that it is likely the user is obtaining the money illegally by selling drugs or by prostitution.

The profit margin on drugs is high. For example, three countries grow all the coca leaves—Columbia, Peru, and Bolivia—where a kilogram of processed cocaine sells for between $585 and $780 a kilogram (2.2 lbs.) (Stewart 2013). By the time it is imported to the United States, distributed, and diluted, the end user pays $150,000 per kilo (Woody 2016).

I propose that we establish licensed drug outlets in a manner similar to the licensed alcohol outlets in Canada. Drugs would be tested in certified labs and labeled accurately to identify the potency of the active ingredients to reduce the chance of an accidental overdose. Legal restrictions might include age limits or concentrations of the active ingredient or limitations on quantity of purchase if overuse has contributed to harm such as auto accidents, physical violence, or health complications. Users of addictive drugs would have an ID card with a smart chip that records purchase to monitor frequency and quantity of use, and they would have a clean needle exchange to reduce the spread of HIV and hepatitis.

The intent of this proposal is to deny organized crime $100 billion of drug profits, reduce the corrupting influence on police and politicians, stop drug wars in other countries, provide help to those abusing drugs, and fund some of the projects proposed elsewhere in this book (see #Paying for New Programs).

Research on Better Drugs

One of the chief concerns about drug use is the deleterious effect of frequent use. A study by the Global Drug Survey found that mushrooms were the safest recreational drug, with 0.2 percent of users reporting need for emergency medical attention compared with 4.8 percent for meth and 0.9 percent for marijuana (Winstock, et al. 2017). Federal clinics could provide information about relative drug safety to users based on such information and develop recreational drugs that have fewer harmful side effects.

I propose that we shift some of our research funding to support the development of safer recreational drugs.

Criminalize Profiting from Sex by Another Person

Another large source of income for organized crime is sex in the form of prostitution and human trafficking. A 2013 study of prostitution in 150 countries concluded that "countries where prostitution is legal experience larger reported human trafficking inflows" (Cho 2013). In 1999, Sweden passed a law that shifted the onus of prostitution to the buyer making it illegal to buy sex. The "Swedish model" has been adopted by Norway (2008), Iceland (2009), and Canada (2014) (Goldberg 2014). The results in Sweden have been dramatic:

> *"We have significantly less prostitution than our neighboring countries, even if we take into account the fact that some of it happens underground," says*

> *Trolle. "We only have between 105 and 130 women—both on the Internet and on the street— active (in prostitution) in Stockholm today. In Oslo, it's 5,000."*

> *Another benefit of the ban is that hardly any country in the European Union has fewer problems with human trafficking. According to the Swedish police, 400 to 600 foreign women are brought to Sweden each year to be prostitutes. In Finland, which is only half the size of Sweden, that number is between 10,000 and 15,000 women. (Anwar 2007)*

The Canadians adopted this approach in 2014:

> *This shift in the approach to prostitution is clearly evident in the Preamble of Bill C-36 which states: "Parliament of Canada recognizes the social harm caused by the objectification of the human body and the commodification of sexual activity."*

The Preamble also highlights the goals of the new legislation to:

> *Protect human dignity and the equality of all Canadians by discouraging prostitution, which has a disproportionate impact on women and children*

> *Denounce and prohibit the purchase of sexual services because it creates a demand for prostitution*

> *Encourage those who engage in prostitution to report incidents of violence and to leave prostitution.*

Another indicator of this fundamental paradigm shift is the location of the new offences in the Criminal Code. Previously, all prostitution related offences were located in Part VII of the Criminal Code—Disorderly Houses, Gaming and Betting. The new offences targeting the purchasers of sexual services and pimps will be located in Part VIII of the Criminal Code—Offences Against the Person and Reputation. This is a distinct acknowledgement that the act of buying sexual services is an offence against another individual. Research shows that buying sexual services is most often carried out on individuals who have no real freedom. It is an offence against the most vulnerable individuals in our society who are enslaved by a violent pimp, poverty or drug addiction. (Smith 2014)

I like the effectiveness of the Swedish model except that it still criminalizes one of the two people engaged in the act but not the criminal enterprise behind human trafficking. I think that two adults should be able to contract for sex if neither is being coerced and that the primary problems with prostitution are human trafficking and coercion. We can adopt a part of the Swedish model that takes advantage of the years of experience the Swedes and the Canadians have accumulated to reduce the criminal income from human trafficking and combine it with a licensing program to protect the rights of women and the health of both buyers and sellers of sex.

I propose that we license sexual commerce where neither party to the transaction is a criminal. To obtain a license to sell sex, the applicant for the license must show that the seller is of legal age and resident of the state. Sale of sex could take place in licensed locations that would provide common services such as billing, scheduling, and security. Sellers of sex would rent space in those facilities and pay a reasonable rent for the space and services. Licensed sellers would be required to take periodic health examinations and account for earnings and pay taxes. They would have the protection of the police from human traffickers or violence from customers. The income from the sale of sex would be owned by the seller. Transfer of income to a third party such as a pimp or madam would be illegal. This shifts the focus of law enforcement on to the people who kidnap, coerce, entrap, and transport women and children for profit.

The purpose of this proposal is to make it illegal to profit from a sexual transaction between other people, substantially reduce the tragedy of human trafficking, and divert the income from organized crime to other programs mentioned elsewhere in this book.

Payday Loans
Those of us who are relatively wealthy are often unaware of what it is like to live on the edge financially. I would see a building in a poor part of town advertising a check-cashing service, and I didn't understand why someone would pay a service fee to get his or her paycheck cashed when it was a free service if you had a checking account. It didn't occur to me that they didn't have enough money to maintain a minimum balance in a checking account.

An article in the *Atlantic* was a wake-up call that explained that it isn't just poor people who are living with no financial margin (Gabler 2016). In the article, the author quoted a study by the Federal Reserve that said 47 percent of Americans couldn't come up with $400 in an emergency. This percentage increased to more than 66 percent for households with income less than $40,000 a year, and 20 percent have no bank account (Report on the Economic Well-Being of U.S. Households in 2014 2014). This lack of reserve money makes many people vulnerable to illegal loan-sharking and extraordinarily high fees, such as a bank charging a fifty-dollar fee for a one-day overdraft on a checking account.

I propose that we provide those who participate in national service a small stock fund that pays dividends. Owners could choose to take up to $500 of the accumulated dividend to meet short-term needs. The principal of the stock fund would not be available until the owner reached retirement age (see <u>Create a Culture of Service and Higher Education</u>).

The purpose of this proposal is to reduce charging economically vulnerable people exceedingly high interest rates and to provide those people with a greater sense of security.

Take the Profit Out of Buying Politicians

Another form of corruption has become common. Members of Congress raised more than a billion dollars for the 2014 election (O'Donnell 2016). When a congressperson is told that he or she must raise $18,000 a day, it is easy to see how there is a strong likelihood that donors with money will have undue influence on the way congresspersons vote.

Laws that were intended to limit large contributions from individuals and organizations have not been effective. The most recent development has been the expenditure of corporate profits to influence elections. One way to approach the problem is to ask what economic benefits corporations expect from their donations and seek ways to reduce them, thereby reducing the incentive for corporations to spend money buying politicians.

The government controls corporations using a stick-and-carrot approach—regulation and tax reductions. Regulations are direct orders on what the corporation must or must not do and might be enforced by fines while tax reductions, which are also called "breaks" or "loopholes," are intended to provide incentives to voluntarily do what the government wants.

End Most Corporate Tax Deductions and Lower the Rates

In 1913, Congress ratified the Sixteenth Amendment, which authorized the income tax:

> *The Congress shall have power to lay and collect taxes on incomes, from whatever source derived, without apportionment among the several States, and without regard to any census or enumeration. (Sixteenth Amendment n.d.)*

Politicians have also discovered that they can buy votes from the electorate by giving tax reductions for spending on items like mortgage interest, childcare, charitable giving, and employer-paid health-care benefits. It sounds like free money, but the result is a higher tax rate and a much more complicated tax code.

The US tax code is extraordinarily complex, and just filling out the tax forms takes individuals and corporations 6.1 billion hours of labor and $31.7 billion for tax-preparation assistance (Tasselmyer 2015). That's an average of eighteen hours and ninety-eight dollars per person for every man, woman, and child in the United States.

The idea of influencing decisions and behavior by rewarding them with tax reductions reduces the income of the government and the amount of money it has for its programs, but the bigger problem is that corporations have discovered that they can buy tax reductions by spending money electing politicians who will vote for the tax reduction. If the corporation gets to write the specific tax law, they can give themselves a tax reduction but not their rivals. This practice insures that all the rival corporations spend money buying politicians so they don't end up with a competitive disadvantage.

In my opinion, a role of government is to provide a level playing field of regulations and taxes on which corporations can compete. The corporate-tax rate at 39 percent in the United States is already higher than other developed countries with whom those corporations must compete that have an average tax rate of 24 percent. After most large corporations subtract the numerous deductions allowed in the current tax code, the effective US corporate-tax rate is about 27 percent (Tsang 2014).

Another problem with this tax system is the way it can distort market forces, which is addressed under the topic of health care (see #Reorganize Health Care).

I suggest that it is time to abandon this approach to government because it has led to corruption of our elected officials.

                    Take the Profit Out of Buying Politicians

I propose that we eliminate almost all tax reductions. An exception would be tax deferments such as retirement accounts where the tax is collected but at a later date and other taxes. This would be accompanied by a reduction of the corporate-tax rate from 39 percent to 27 percent—about what they are effectively paying now and that is more competitive with other developed countries. Personal income tax deductions would also be eliminated, and the tax rates lowered to the effective rate. Even though the rates are lowered, the income to the government would remain the same while saving taxpayers the time and cost of preparing their tax returns.

The intention of this proposal is to reduce the value of spending money on buying politicians by corporations, to reduce the time wasted preparing tax returns, and to level the playing field for corporations to compete with each other and with foreign companies.

Office of Fair Business Regulations
Another reason for corporations to spend large amounts of money electing politicians is to change regulations on issues like product liability, worker safety, and environmental protection. This type of influence is hard to track because the special consideration might be buried in hundreds of pages of documents.

I propose that we create an Office of Fair Business Regulations (OFBR). One of the purposes of this office is to assure that new regulations do not give one company an unfair advantage over another US company. They would also oversee regulations from various agencies to assure that regulations from different agencies do not contradict or duplicate each other and reduce cost of compliance.

Require Shareholder Rebates for Political Donations
Since the Citizens United ruling by the Supreme Court, corporations are free to use corporate funds to buy advertising that supports issues and individual candidates. Justice Kennedy's majority opinion said that corporate spending on political campaigns would be limited by the votes of shareholders (Raskin 2014):

> *The Government contends further that corporate*
> *independent expenditures can be limited because of its*

> *interest in protecting dissenting shareholders from being compelled to fund corporate political speech. This asserted interest, like Austin's antidistortion rationale, would allow the Government to ban the political speech even of media corporations. See supra, at 35–37. Assume, for example, that a shareholder of a corporation that owns a newspaper disagrees with the political views the newspaper expresses. See Austin, 494 U. S., at 687 (SCALIA, J., dissenting). Under the Government's view, that potential disagreement could give the Government the authority to restrict the media corporation's political speech. The First Amendment does not allow that power. **There is, furthermore, little evidence of abuse that cannot be corrected by shareholders "through the procedures of corporate democracy."** Bellotti, 435 U. S., at 794; see id., at 794, n. 34. (Citizens United v. Federal Election Commission 2009)*

It would be a reasonable assumption that CEOs could not spend shareholder money for a candidate over the objections of a majority of shareholders if the shareholders knew about it. Here are four aspects of this situation to consider:

- Corporate donations can be hidden from shareholders (Dunbar 2012).
- Money spent on political campaigns is diverted from paying dividends or increasing stock value.
- Minority stockholders would be supporting a candidate or issue against their wishes with their money.

I propose that publicly owned companies be required to allow shareholders to vote on whether to authorize the CEO to spend their money on political campaigns. Shareholders who vote no would receive a dividend check as compensation whenever the CEO spent corporate money on politics.

                Require Shareholder Rebates for Political Donations

For example, if a publicly owned corporation spends $1 million on political activities and 30 percent of its stock is owned by nonpolitical investors, the corporation would have to issue a dividend of $300,000 to its nonpolitical investors or compensate them with additional stock of the same value.

Chapter Five

Council of Economic and Financial Advisors

Our government was designed with the understanding that men are not angels:

> *If men were angels, no government would be necessary. If angels were to govern men, neither external nor internal controls on government would be necessary. In framing a government which is to be administered by men over men, the great difficulty lies in this: you must first enable the government to control the governed; and in the next place oblige it to control itself. (Madison 1787)*

Madison went on to explain in Federalist Paper #51 that the government should consist of independent branches of government where the greed and ambition of men could balance and check each other. This system has served us well except where it comes to finance and the economy. Efforts to deregulate the economy and its financial institutions and leave its controls in the hands of well-meaning people has failed as demonstrated in 2008. The chair of the Federal Reserve during the 2008 financial crisis, Alan Greenspan, admitted to Congress:

> *I made a mistake in presuming that the self-interests of organizations, specifically banks and others, were such that they were best capable of protecting their own shareholders and their equity in the firms. (Greenspan - I Was Wrong About the Economy. Sort of 2008)*

Greenspan evidently thought that the banks and investment houses were run by intelligent, thoughtful, responsible people (angels) rather than the men whom Madison knew.

Here are some of the failings of our financial system in recent years.

Major Financial Failures

The old saying applies here: "If something is too good to be true, it probably isn't." In my lifetime, I have witnessed several major financial problems, and in the process of doing the research for this book, I've become aware of a few more.

S&L Failure

Saving and Loan (S&L) institutions were created by Congress to provide low-cost home mortgages. In 1980, S&Ls provided about half of the home mortgage loans in the United States. A bank or S&L makes money on home loans by taking in deposits on which they pay the depositor interest and then loaning the money out for home mortgages at a higher interest rate. The difference in the two interest rates pays for the administrative costs and the profits of the bank or S&L. The flaws in the system were that the loans are for many years at a fixed rate, but the deposits could be withdrawn if a higher-paying investment became available to the depositor and the loans were guaranteed by the US taxpayer.

Inflation in the 1970s was greater than expected, and other investments were paying higher interest rates than deposits in S&Ls. To keep the money in the S&Ls, they started paying higher interest rates for deposits. The result was that they were paying out more for the deposits than the long-term mortgages were bringing in.

The government allowed the S&Ls to make other riskier investments to try to make enough money to offset the losses on the home loans, but that didn't work. Between 1989 and 1995, the government closed 747 S&Ls, which cost the taxpayers about $124 billion. This is about $1,000 per adult taxpayer; however, I did not see a tax increase of $2,000 for my wife and I to pay for this default (Robinson n.d.).

In the decade leading up to the financial crisis of 2008, the government was encouraging, and insuring, home mortgage loans again. Many of the new loans were made to people who did not have enough money to pay part of the mortgage amount to protect the lender from a loss if they had to seize the property for nonpayment. Instead, the US taxpayers were forced to assume significant portions of the risk. These loans were called *subprime* because they weren't as safe as prime mortgages. Increase in demand fueled by the availability of these loans caused home prices to rise. Loan companies bundled these subprime mortgages together and used them as collateral for other loans based on the assumption that house prices would always go up. Rating agencies like Moody's and S&P gave these bundles AAA ratings, as if they were the safest possible investment.

Eventually, the prices of homes stopped rising, and people tried to sell their homes, which caused prices to fall. Because borrowers did not have much equity in their houses, the selling price soon became less than the amount they owed on the mortgage. People who sold would have no house and no money to put down on another house and would still have a mortgage payment!

Because these loans were used to collateralize other loans, a cascade took place that caused the financial crisis of 2008. The result was an economic depression that cost the country between "a few trillion dollars to over $10 trillion" (Financial Regulatory Reform: Financial Crisis Losses and Potential Impacts of the Dodd-Frank Act 2013). Instead of an increase in taxes, this crisis might have cost you your job or you might owe more on your house than you can sell it for. Assuming a cost of about $6 trillion, the average direct and indirect cost to the 122 million people who pay personal federal income tax would be about $50,000 each. Fortunately, this crisis did not cost me my job or affect my pension, but the value of my house did go down about $100,000. After ten years, my house value is back up to about what I paid for it. The companies—S&P Global and Moody's—that rated these bundles as AAA that cost the country about $6 trillion were fined. S&P paid $1.5 billion, and Moody's paid

$864 million (Moody's $864m Penalty for Ratings in Run-up to 2008 Financial Crisis 2017); (Viswanatha and Freifeld 2015). The people who were supposed to safeguard us did not and paid less than .04 percent of the cost ($2.3 billion/$6 trillion) to our economy.

Military Spending without Auditable Accounting
The budget of the Department of Defense (DOD) was $597 billion in 2016 or $4,893 per taxpayer (Taylor and Karklis 2016). I was surprised to learn that unlike other branches of government, the military has not been able to account for the money it spends in a way that can be audited:

> *DOD financial management was first added to our High-Risk List in 1995. Long-standing, uncorrected deficiencies with DOD's financial management systems, business processes, financial manager qualifications, and material internal control and financial reporting weaknesses continue to negatively affect DOD's ability to manage the department and make sound decisions on mission and operations. Having sound financial management practices and reliable, useful, and timely financial and performance information is important to help ensure accountability over DOD's extensive resources and efficiently and economically manage the department's assets and budgets. This is particularly important because DOD's reported discretionary spending makes up about half of the federal government's reported discretionary spending, and its reported assets represent more than 70 percent of the federal government's reported physical assets. However, DOD remains one of the few federal entities that cannot demonstrate its ability to accurately account for and reliably report its spending or assets. DOD's financial management problems remain one of three major impediments preventing us from expressing an opinion on the consolidated financial statements of the federal government. (GAO High Risk List 2017)*

In 2013, Reuters News published a story that described how the navy adjusted its accounts each year so that its books balanced—at least on paper. Each time an *adjustment* was made, it had ripple effects in other accounts. In 2015, a similar report showed that there was a total of $6.5 trillion adjustments in the 2015 army budget out of only $587 billion for the entire military. This implies that for every dollar Congress allocated for military spending in 2015, there were at least $10 of "adjustments" (Paltrow 2016). Congress has ordered the Department of Defense to update its accounting methods to make them auditable by 2017.

In brief, the Department of Defense (DOD) has no idea how much is being wasted or stolen, and this is not widely known or reported (see #Audit the Military).

Little Savings or Home Equity

My wife was a banker for twenty-seven years, and she was very proud of her profession and how important bankers were to the fabric of the community. She was disturbed in 1999 when the banking laws were changed. Formerly under the 1933 Banking Act, also known as the Glass-Steagall Act, commercial banks that held your life savings and loaned it out carefully to build community businesses were not allowed to invest your money in stocks. That changed in 1999 when the law was repealed. My wife told me that the bank's culture changed from a service culture to a sales culture. Managers in her bank were rewarded for approving loans with much greater risk levels than ever before. The risky loans were bundled and sold, so the bank issuing the risky loan got its money back and someone else assumed the risk. The level of risk was supposed to be rated by an independent agency. They were into maximizing the bank's profits rather than protecting their depositor's assets.

I was raised with the idea that you borrow money to buy a home and then pay off the loan by the time you retire so you can live on a reduced income because you have no mortgage payment. I recall my surprise when I saw a sign in my wife's bank that said, "I found $20,000 in my attic!" It was an advertisement for a home equity loan. The implication was that this was free money that you could spend on that dream vacation without regard to your old age or retirement. I commented to my wife, "I thought my banker was supposed to be my trusted financial advisor. Spending my home equity without regard for the future is a bad idea."

An article in the *Atlantic* caught my attention last year when it proclaimed that almost half of Americans (47 percent) couldn't come up with $400 in an emergency without selling something or borrowing (Gabler 2016). I am blessed with a good income, and I've saved enough of it to feel financially secure, so it was hard for me to believe this. However, at a recent dinner party that I gave in Charleston, South Carolina, I related this statement and was surprised to hear that two of the five guests confirmed that they were in that situation even though both of them are well educated (they have significant health-care expenses).

The median savings—including home equity—of a person in their sixties is $172,000. If you are accustomed to a salary of $60,000 a year (Parker 2016), that is less than three years of retirement income. Increasingly, people are depending on Social Security for their retirement income rather than their own savings (see #Social Security Trust Funds). Present laws encourage savings for retirement by offering tax deferments. These incentives have little impact on those who either pay no tax or are in the lower tax brackets (Parker 2016). We have been encouraged to spend our savings by the very people who should have been advising us to build equity in our homes for retirement due to this change in banking law.

Income Concentration

The tax and income structure of the United States has changed dramatically since the 1980s to favor the wealthy. Since the 1980s, the income of the top 1 percent has tripled from $428,000 to $1,300,000, while the bottom 50 percent remained the same at $16,000 (Long 2016) (see #Income Inequality).

The year following the first Gulf War in 1991 while my wife and I were doing our taxes, I said to her, "We haven't gotten a bill for the Gulf War." The Department of Defense estimated the cost of the first Gulf War to be $61 billion (Gulf War Fast Facts 2016). Since there are about 122 million adults who pay personal federal income tax, our share would have been about $500 each or $1,000 for the two of us (Barro 2012). Since our taxes didn't go up by $1,000, the money came from somewhere else, but I don't recall anyone explaining where they got the money. It was great television with practically no casualties on our side—and it was free!

Airport and Airway Trust Fund

Several years ago, there was discussion of a new tax to pay for upgrading the radar and navigation system for commercial airliners. A colleague of mine who worked in the aviation industry told me that every airline ticket and gallon of jet fuel have been taxed for years to build up a trust fund for just this purpose—the Airport & Airway Trust Fund (AATF). The problem, he explained, is that the government borrowed the money and spent it on other things—the trust fund was empty except for worthless IOUs.

I forgot about his claim until I read that the government plans to deploy the system this year, so I looked into the issue. First, let's be clear about the term *trust fund*. According to Investopedia:

> *A trust fund is a fund comprised of a variety of assets intended to provide benefits to an individual or organization. A grantor establishes a trust fund to provide financial security to an individual, most often a child or grandchild, or organizations, such as a charity or other nonprofit organization. (Trust Fund n.d.)*

The key concept here is that the fund is comprised of assets that have real value such as property, stock, or gold coins in a mattress that could be sold when cash is needed. Instead of assets, the Aviation Trust Fund has $13.4 billion of "**nonmarketable** par value Treasury Certificates of Indebtedness":

The Secretary of the Treasury invests AATF funds on behalf of the FAA. The FAA investments are considered investment authority and are available to offset the cost of operations to the extent authorized by Congress. As of September 30, 2016...$13.4 billion...billion were invested respectively in U.S. Treasury Certificates of Indebtedness. Nonmarketable par value Treasury Certificates of Indebtedness are special series debt securities issued by the Bureau of Fiscal Services to federal accounts, and are purchased and redeemed at par (face value) exclusively through the Federal Investment Branch of the U.S. Treasury's Bureau of Fiscal Services. (FAA 2016 Performance & Accountability Report 2016)

My friend explained that another branch of the government borrows the money from the trust fund, spends it, and leaves the trust fund holding an IOU. This type of loan is called *intragovernmental debt*.

Intergovernmental debt is like loaning money to your brother-in-law who can't manage his money but who insists that his I.O.U. is good because his sister is married to a rich guy—you!

To collect on the $13.4 billion in debt to pay for a new airline navigation system, the other government agencies would have to come up with money they've already spent. Their only source of income is the taxpayer, so they would have to raise taxes, borrow the money, or pay back the loan from their current budget. The AAFT might as well do that itself because the $13.4 billion in fees that were collected from ticket sales and jet fuel is gone. The NextGen airways system is being paid for out of current cash flow plus additional fees paid by the airlines, which will eventually be passed on to the passengers instead of spending the $13 billion that should already be there from past fees (Michaels 2009).

Learning that the $13 billion in the Airport & Airways Trust Fund was gone would account for $110 per taxpayer (assuming 122 million federal income taxpayers) out of the $500 spent on the Gulf War, so I still didn't know where the other $390 came from.

Social Security Trust Funds

Learning that the money in the Airport & Airways Trust Fund was gone provided a background for understanding the condition of much larger trust funds—Social Security and Medicare/Medicaid.

The Social Security Trust Fund consists of two trust funds, the Federal Old-Age and Survivors Insurance Trust Fund and Federal Disability Insurance Trust Fund. In 1983, a bill with bipartisan support increased the payroll tax to build up a fund that would be there when the baby-boom generation began to retire in 2010. Since then, the program has collected $19 trillion in taxes and paid out $16.1 trillion in benefits. The difference (a bit more than $2.8 trillion) supposedly went into the trust fund (A Summary of the 2016 Annual Reports 2016).

The Social Security Administration tells us that the trust funds are backed by bonds that have the full faith and credit of the US government. These are not marketable treasury bonds but the same intergovernmental bonds in the Airport & Airways Trust Fund. The debate over the status of the retirement trust fund has been contentious. One side maintains that loaning the money to other branches of government is the only practical use for the money. The alternative would be for the government to own enormous amounts of stock, buildings, or land.

The argument that I find persuasive was made in *Forbes* magazine by Merrill Matthews. In 2011, Congress threatened to withhold approval of raising the debt ceiling. In response, President Obama told the nation that Social Security checks would not go out if the debt ceiling was not raised (Holan and Jacobson 2011). Matthews argues that this statement proves that the Social Security

Trust Fund does not have any real value; otherwise money could have been taken from the trust fund to make the payments (Matthews 2011).

Now that the baby-boom generation is retiring, the predicted shortfall in cash flow is occurring. Since 2010, the amount collected in payroll taxes for Social Security has been less than the amount paid out. Instead of dipping into the trust fund that was created to meet this need, we are borrowing the money—hence the need to raise the debt ceiling. The evidence is convincing—like the Airport & Airways trust fund, the Social Security Trust Fund does not have any assets of value that can be converted into cash to pay retirement checks. The money we are paying out to retirees each year is the money that workers are paying into the fund—the money we paid into the fund since 1983 has been spent.

To get an idea of how much $2.8 trillion is, consider that the market value of all the gold in Fort Knox and other US depositories is only worth $345.8 billion (Status Report of the U.S. Government Gold Reserve 2017). There are about 234 million adults in the United States who are paying or have paid into this retirement system, so the trust fund amount that has been spent is about $12,000 each.

As of December 31, 2014, intragovernmental debt holdings are owed to the following trust funds (in millions of dollars): (Schedule of Federal Debt 2014)

SSA: Federal-Old Age & Survivors Insurance Trust Fund	$2,729,270
OPM: Civil Service Retirement and Disability Fund	845,419
DOD: Military Retirement Fund	540,698
HHS: DOD Medicare-Eligible Retiree Health Care Fund	208,077
DOD: Federal Hospital Insurance Trust Fund	197,887
SSA: Federal Supplementary Medical Insurance Trust Fund	69,099
HHS: Federal Disability Insurance Trust Fund	60,311

DOE: Nuclear Waste Disposal Fund	51,588
OPM: Deposit Insurance Fund	50,739
FDIC: Postal Service Retiree Health Benefits Fund	49,233
OPM: Employees Life Insurance Fund	43,681
DOL: Unemployment Trust Fund	34,471
OPM: Employees' Health Benefits Fund	22,772
Treasury: Exchange Stabilization Fund	22,648
DOS: Pension Benefit Guaranty Corporation	19,214
DOL: Foreign Service Retirement and Disability Fund	17,972
DOT: Airport and Airway Trust Fund	13,352
NCUA: National Credit Union Share Insurance Fund	11,344
Other Programs and Funds	115,612
Total	5,103,387

Now I see where the government got the money for the Gulf wars and the wars in Iraq and Afghanistan.

GAO Report: High-Risk Areas

The US Government Accountability Office (GAO) tries to draw attention to financial problems that need attention by publishing a High Risk List every two years. The list for 2017 is as follows:

- Improving Federal Management of Programs that Serve Tribes and Their Members—NEW
- U.S. Government's Environmental Liability—NEW
- 2020 Decennial Census—NEW
- Strategic Human Capital Management
- Managing Federal Real Property
- Funding the Nation's Surface Transportation System
- Modernizing the U.S. Financial Regulatory System and the Federal Role in Housing Finance
- Restructuring the U.S. Postal Service to Achieve Sustainable Financial Viability
- Management of Federal Oil and Gas Resources
- Limiting the Federal Government's Fiscal Exposure by Better Managing Climate Change Risks
- Improving the Management of IT Acquisitions and Operations
- DOD Supply Chain Management
- DOD Weapon Systems Acquisition

- DOD Financial Management
- DOD Business Systems Modernization
- DOD Support Infrastructure Management
- DOD Approach to Business Transformation
- Ensuring the Security of Federal Information Systems and Cyber Critical Infrastructure and Protecting the Privacy of Personally Identifiable Information
- Strengthening Department of Homeland Security Management Functions
- Ensuring the Effective Protection of Technologies Critical to U.S. National Security Interests
- Improving Federal Oversight of Food Safety
- Protecting Public Health through Enhanced Oversight of Medical Products
- Transforming EPA's Process for Assessing and Controlling Toxic Chemicals
- Mitigating Gaps in Weather Satellite Data
- DOE's Contract Management for the National Nuclear Security Administration and Office of Environmental Management
- NASA Acquisition Management
- DOD Contract Management
- Enforcement of Tax Laws
- Medicare Program
- Medicaid Program
- Improving and Modernizing Federal Disability Programs
- Pension Benefit Guaranty Corporation Insurance Programs
- National Flood Insurance Program
- Managing Risks and Improving VA Health Care

The GAO has no authority to deal with these issues; it can only alert Congress to the problems.

Council of Economic and Financial Advisors
Given the list of financial, monetary, and economic problems the country has experienced in recent decades, I think it is time to recognize that our three branches of government do not have the

necessary checks and balances. We need a fourth branch of government to change the balance of power from a three-legged stool to a four-legged chair.

I propose that we create the Council of Economic and Financial Advisors (COE) that could propose laws through the House of Representatives related to financial, monetary, and economic regulations.

The COE would have the following makeup, procedures and powers:

- The council will consist of nine members with eighteen-year tenures, staggered so that a replacement is needed at least every two years.
- When a position becomes vacant, the president chooses three candidates who have top credentials in their field such as former heads of the Security and Exchange Commission (SEC), the Federal Reserve, and the Congressional Budget Office (COB) or Nobel Prize winners in economics.
- The Senate has sixty days to pick one of them; otherwise the president makes the choice from those three to fill the vacant seat.
- Members of the COE propose new regulations or changes to existing laws related to economic, financial, and monetary issues. If a simple majority of the COE approves, the proposal becomes a bill and is forwarded to the appropriate House of Representatives subcommittee, bypassing the rules committee, (see Weekend Election Day) along with majority and minority opinions written by members of the COE.
- The House subcommittee debates and votes on the proposed bill. The bill may be voted out of subcommittee for a vote by the full House, or it may be sent back to the COE with an explanation of why it was rejected.
- The COE may revise the bill and resubmit it to the House subcommittee, or if there is a two-thirds majority of the COE, the bill can be sent directly to the floor of the House for a mandatory vote, bypassing the subcommittee.

- If the bill passes the House, it is treated like any other bill that passes the House, that is, it must pass the Senate and be signed by the president and is subject to review by the courts.

The intent of this proposal is to provide expert input on financial and economic policies that are less influenced by politics and force the house to debate and vote on them providing a fourth, stabilizing leg of government.

Balance the Budget with a Value-Added Tax

It has become an annual question of whether to raise the debt ceiling or default on our loans. This debate misses the primary point that the government is spending more each year than it is taking in. Politicians often tell us they can solve our money problems by taking money from someone else. It is time we recognize that we need to balance our spending with additional taxation on consumption such as a Goods and Services Tax (GST), which is also known as a value-added tax (VAT).

The VAT is used by 140 countries, including almost all developed countries except the United States. It is a form of sales tax that is collected at each stage of production of a product. Most countries use a *narrow base* that exempts food, education, and health care. The remaining goods and services that would be subject to the tax amount to about 46 percent of household consumption. According to the Congressional Budget Office, a 5 percent VAT on a narrow base would raise about $190 billion (Impose a 5 Percent Value-Added Tax 2016). Many people, including most criminals, hide their income from the IRS and avoid paying income tax, but those people would pay the VAT each time they buy something with their income.

The difference between the government's spending and tax revenue is about $443 billion (2017 United States Budget Estimate 2017). Each year, we borrow this money and obligate our children to repay it. For example, in 2017, Congress voted to provide relief to hurricane victims at the same time they agreed to raise the debt ceiling.

Providing disaster relief by raising the debt limit and borrowing the money would be like taking out a loan to help your neighbor recover from a flood, but instead of paying for the loan yourself, you obligate the children of both your families to pay back the loan.

We need to restore the relationship between spending and taxation in the minds of the people.

I propose that we institute a VAT of about 11 percent or 12 percent. The amount of the VAT would be tied to our spending. If we decide to send more troops into another country or pay for hurricane relief, the extra spending would be paid for the next year by an increase in the VAT. Conversely, if the Congress acts to reduce spending and balance the budget, the VAT would go down to zero or to a minimum that could be applied toward reducing the deficit (see Tax-Return Voting).

If the median household makes $56,500 and a VAT of 11.6 percent is applied to 46 percent of that, the household would pay $3,000 in VAT, and it would balance the budget. It would be part of the price of the goods and services we consume like a sales tax.

Balance the Budget with a Value-Added Tax

Chapter Six

Income Inequality

I recall that one of my favorite comic book characters as a child was Scrooge McDuck. Scrooge was Donald Duck's rich uncle who had so much money he kept it in a money bin the size of a building and went swimming in it. Scrooge got his money by being smart and resourceful, not lucky or by inheriting it. I was raised with the idea that the way to manage money was to save ten percent, give ten percent, risk ten percent, and learn to live happily with thanksgiving on the rest. My parents started several small businesses. Some failed, some provided us with a good living, and a few made enough extra money to pay for my college education.

In the late 70s and early 80s, fortunes were being made by young entrepreneurs in the computer business. I decided to take a big risk with the hope of becoming rich. I quit my safe job as a tenured high school teacher, cashed in my retirement equity, and started a software company with my best friend. It didn't work out as planned and I lost my investment, but it lead to a better teaching job at a university. In the 90s and early 2000s I took another chance and started writing college textbooks on how to use personal computers. This time I didn't quit my primary job and did the writing at night and on weekends with the same friend and my wife. The first several books didn't make much but eventually we worked our way up to some of the publisher's best-selling titles. About a half-million students have used textbooks that I helped write. I don't have a money bin, but I now own a very nice home on a lake that is paid for and we are enjoying a financially secure retirement.

For some of my liberal friends, the idea of income inequality is inherently bad because they believe that everyone should be equal while my conservative friends often say that the opportunity to become wealthy is the American dream and that America's poor have about the same standard of living as the poor in European countries and the gap in America is due to greater wealth at the top (Worstall 2013).

I'm all for the American dream of achieving wealth for people who risk their own time and money and build something that creates value. I'm less empathetic toward people who didn't risk anything and just inherited great wealth, found a way to divert a portion of other people's money, or vote themselves large salaries for managing companies that others built. I refer to that type of income as *unearned income*.

In this chapter, we consider some ways to limit the accumulation of wealth through unearned income.

Link Minimum Wage to CEO Income Tax

From the 1930s through the 1970s, the average CEO income was about $1 million, adjusted for inflation, and rose to just under $2 million by the end of the 1980s. Prior to 1993, CEO pay was deducted from corporation profits as an expense. In 1993, the tax code was changed to cap company deductions for CEO pay at 1 million but had no cap for performance-based income like stock options. Since that ruling, average CEO compensation, including performance pay, jumped to 9.2 million by the end of 2005 (Frydman 2010) (see #Take the Profit Out of Buying Politicians). By 2015, average CEO compensation for S&P 500 companies rose to $13.8 million (Chamberlain 2015). See Figure 2.

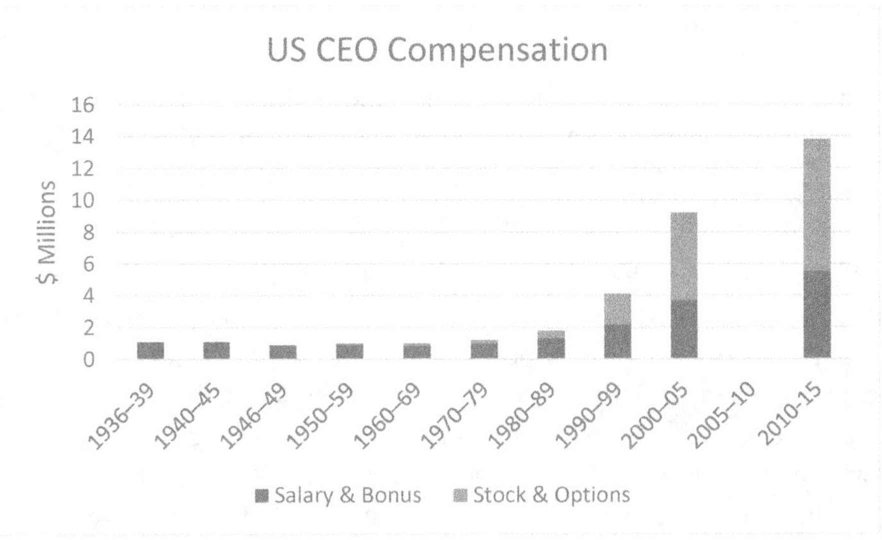

Figure 2

In 2015, the Securities and Exchange Commission passed a rule that requires a public company to disclose the ratio of CEO compensation to the median compensation of employees (U.S. Securities and Exchange Commission 2015). Preliminary estimates are available that show 338 of the S&P 500 company CEOs are paid more than one hundred times the median pay of workers in their respective companies (Chamberlain 2015).

The city of Portland, Oregon, adopted a business income surtax of 10 percent on those companies whose CEOs receive compensation greater than 100 times the median employee income and 25 percent if they exceed 250 times the median employee income. City officials estimate the new tax would generate between $2.5 and $3.5 million per year (Morgenson 2016).

Identifying which companies have the greatest disparity is useful, but I don't think Portland's measure will have the desired effect for two reasons: first, they use the median pay rather than the lowest pay. The median income is the middle value, not the average or the lowest. For example, if a company had only five employees and pay levels were $20,000, $30,000, $40,000, $50,000, and $10,000,000, the median (middle value) is $40,000 (two higher and two lower). If you gave the person at the bottom a raise to $25,000, the median would not change. Second, the penalty is on the company. The surcharge can be passed on to consumers or shareholders without affecting the people making the decisions.

I propose that the maximum personal federal income tax be set at 75 percent for CEOs, top corporate executives, and the members of their compensation committees who set CEO compensation packages that exceed one hundred times the *lowest* paid worker, including contracted workers. The present top tax bracket for those earning over $415,050 is 39.6 percent. The tax would be triggered if the CEO is compensated at more than one hundred times the lowest paid wage of an employee or of a contractor's employees. In the case of part-time workers, the full-time equivalent would be used. For example, if a part-time worker is paid $9.31 an hour and works thirty hours a week for fifty-one weeks, their annual pay would be $14,244. If they worked at that wage for forty hours a week, it would be $19,000. The CEO and members of the compensation board would pay a tax of 75 percent on their income over $1,900,000.

For example, the CEO of Chipolte, Steve Ellis, received $28,924,00 in compensation in 2014 while the median (not lowest) worker received $19,000 (Chamberlain 2015). In this example, we will assume that $19,000 is also the lowest wage, and Ellis received $27,000,000 above the 100× limit on which he would pay 75 percent instead 39.6 percent. This would cost him an extra $9,558,000 in taxes. If he decided to raise the minimum wage at Chipolte by $1/hour, his lowest paid workers would earn an extra $2,000. As a result, an additional $200,000 of his income would be taxed at the lower rate, and he would keep $70,000 ($200,000 x (75%-39.6%)).

In general, if this proposal were adopted, for every $1/hour wage increase the CEO granted his lowest paid employees, he would personally gain $70,000 in tax reduction if he or she is already earning more than 100× the lowest paid worker, which is the case with more than two-thirds of S&P 500 companies.

The intent of this proposal is to directly affect the income of the people who make the decisions on the minimum wage at their companies and incentivize them to share the wealth with their lowest paid workers.

Capital-Gains Tax

There is a difference between wages that you earn yourself and profits from selling an asset for more than you paid for it. The value of the asset might have increased with no effort on your part. Money earned by selling an asset is a *capital gain.*

> *Capital gain is an increase in the value of a capital asset (investment or real estate) that gives it a higher worth than the purchase price. The gain is not realized until the asset is sold. A capital gain may be short-term (one year or less) or long-term.* (Capital Gain n.d.)

It seems to me that there are three different types of capital gain, and they need to be treated differently.

Income from Sale of a Residence

For most people, their greatest asset is their home, and many people live in the same home for years during which time its market price might increase due to inflation or other factors that might not be real income. For example, if you own a house and decide to move, you might sell the house for $30,000 more than the purchase price, but during the time you lived in the house, the price of houses went up by $30,000, so you didn't really increase your income at all if you have to spend that money to buy another comparable home. When a person or couple decides to downsize or move into a rental or senior care facility, the difference between the price of the home and its sale price can be hundreds of thousands of dollars.

Instead of trying to determine how much of the home's increase in value is due to inflation, the Internal Revenue Service (IRS) allows a deduction of up to $500,000 per couple (Topic 701 - Sale of Your Home 2017). If the sale price of the home went up higher than inflation due to other factors like public works projects—paved road, new elementary school, city water and sewer—the homeowner does not pay tax on the extra increase from those public investments.

I propose that the government establish a table of inflation rates of housing prices by geographic region. When someone sells a house for more than he or she paid for it, the table would be used to determine how much of that increase was due to inflation. Homeowners would also be able to deduct money spent on improvements and by the amount paid on the principle of the loan. Because this is a primary source of savings for retirement, I would keep the deduction of $500,000 for a couple and $250,000 for a single person. The amount above either $500,000 or $250,000 after deductions for inflation and improvements would be taxed as income at the appropriate income tax rate.

Investment Property

When my oldest son was only eight years old, his mother and I were anticipating college expenses about ten years in the future. We bought a piece of farmland near a freeway exit within commuting distance of Detroit. The land was a former farmer's field that had been subdivided into ten-acre plots that could not be further subdivided for another ten years. We planned to hold the property for ten years and then subdivide it into one-acre parcels that could be sold individually as home sites. One advantage of this plan was that we would only pay property taxes on its lower value as farmland for the ten years we owned it. A few years after we bought the land, it was discovered that an old gravel pit on the adjoining property had been used as a dump, and leakage from the garbage was contaminating the groundwater that buyers of our property might have to use for their drinking water. We were in danger of losing money on this investment instead of making enough to put our sons through college!

Fortunately, the site qualified as a Superfund site, and the law allowed the government to force one of the contributors to the dump—an auto company—to pay for removal of the waste and determined that the contaminated groundwater was flowing away from our property (Superfund 2017). Our investment was saved, and we made a nice profit. This income was taxed at the capital gains rate, which was lower than our income tax rate. Although I took some risk, the value of the property increased without any work on my part so it was what I call unearned income and should have been taxed as income at my normal rate.

I propose that the government establish a table of inflation rates of investment property prices by geographic region. When someone sells an investment property for more than he or she paid for it, the table would be used to determine how much of that increase was due to inflation. Property owners would also be able to deduct money spent on improvements or principle payments and taxes while they owned the property. The amount after deductions for inflation, improvements, and payments on principle would be taxed as income at the appropriate income tax rate.

Sale of Stocks

People who have more money than they need to live on can invest the extra money by buying real estate or shares in companies (stock). When they sell the stock, if the selling price is higher than they bought it for, the difference is the capital gain. Buying stock in a company is the essence of capitalism, and it provides the money companies need to expand, buy raw materials, and hire people faster than they could if they had to accumulate earnings to do so.

If the selling price of the stock is lower than the amount paid for it, it is a capital loss. If more than one sale takes place in a given year, and some of the sales were for less than the purchase price, the increases and decreases are summed to determine the net capital gain. If the purchase and sale take place within a year of each other, it is a short-term gain, and that gain is taxed at the same rate as other income.

I propose that the profits beyond inflation on long-term capital gains from stocks be taxed at the same rate as other income.

Trust-Fund Loophole

If someone buys a stock for $100 a share and it increases to $400 a share, he or she would have to pay income tax on the difference, minus the amount of inflation. There is an exception to this rule called the *trust-fund loophole*. If the stock is included in a trust fund and is passed on to someone else such as a child, the recipient of the trust fund only pays capital gains on how much the stock increased from when he or she inherited it.

I propose that capital gain from sale of stock that has been inherited in a trust fund be calculated from its date of purchase, not the date of inheritance, and treated like any other capital gain from stocks.

Automation Value Sharing and Universal Income

Remember the Jetsons? In that futuristic cartoon series from 1962 that was revived in 1985 and set in the year 2062, the Jetson family had a robotic maid who did the housework, and George Jetson worked at Spacely Sprockets. A computer named R.U.D.I. (Referential Universal Differential Indexer) at Spacely Sprockets did all of George's work, and George came in for an hour a day, two days a week to turn R.U.D.I on and off. Automation was predicted to make all our lives easier and provide everyone with a high standard of living.

Instead of moving in this direction, companies buy robots to replace workers who do manual labor. Information workers are next when computer programs like IBM's Watson can do many white-collar jobs that are done on a computer. In today's world, George Jetson is either out of a job or working sixty hours a week because companies are reducing workforce instead of sharing the benefits of automation with employees.

A colleague of mine once posed a provocative question: "Why should the company get all the benefit of automation? Why can't three shift workers take out a loan, buy a robot to replace them on the line, and then go home and let the robot do their job while they sit back, collect their paychecks, and enjoy their leisure?"

Another colleague pointed out that in a capitalist economy, the purpose of a company executive is to maximize shareholder value. The problem with that mission is that employees are an expense, and replacing employees with automation serves the purpose of maximizing profits, which leads to income inequality.

Automation is about to make a fundamental change in our lives at the blue-collar and white-collar level, and it will happen so fast that we need to prepare for it in advance. We've all heard about the advent of driverless cars, but the first big challenge will be the economic and social impact of driverless trucks. The technology is already in place to eliminate 2.5 million well-paying truck-driving jobs and several million more jobs for those who support them like restaurant and service-station workers. It will start with platoons of trucks that are controlled by a single driver on the freeways and use of local drivers within the cities like harbor pilots (Driverless Trucks: A Seismic Shift for the Labor Force 2017).

If a job can be done on a computer screen, some of the job can be done by an artificial intelligence. Jobs that involve applying a set of rules such as processing insurance claims, prescribing drugs to match a given diagnosis and checking interactions, and even writing newspaper stories about sports and weather are already done by computers (Alton 2016). The transition probably won't be as rapid as replacing truck drivers, but we are approaching an inflection point in history when we need to revise our basic attitudes toward work.

Corporate profits were about 6 percent in the 1950s through the mid-70s. They went down to about 5 percent in the late '80s through 2000, and then they went up dramatically to about 9 percent in 2006, as shown in Figure 3 (Corporate Profits vs. Gross Domestic Product 2017).

Figure 3

In the same period, wages have gone down as a percent of GDP from 50 percent to 43 percent, as shown in Figure 4 (U.S. Bureau of Economic Analysis 2016).

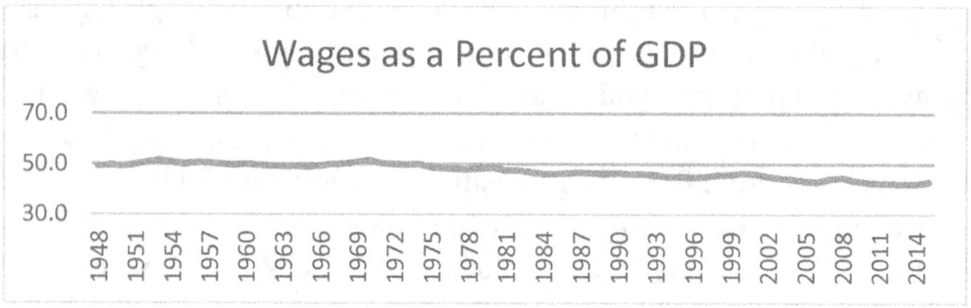

Figure 4

Since the gross domestic product is almost $18 trillion, this 7 percent decrease represents $1.26 trillion that is unearned income for stockholders rather than into wages for workers.

One of the solutions for sharing the wealth of America dates back to a proposal that was sponsored by Richard Nixon—a Republican president—and Patrick Moynihan—a liberal Democratic senator—to co-sponsor a bill to replace welfare with a simple guaranteed income without all the bureaucracy of the welfare program. The proposal passed the House in 1970, but it was defeated in the Senate by a coalition of conservative Democrats and Republicans who wanted a work requirement (Passell and Ross 1973).

The question of how to share America's wealth that is resulting from increased automation with those who do not have well-paid jobs is no longer a question of how to deal with a small fraction of people who don't live near us, but that will affect our unemployed children or ourselves if we get laid off at fifty.

Finland is reviving the idea of a universal income to deal with this problem. They are experimenting with a basic universal income for those who are unemployed of €650 ($725) a month that is not reduced if they take on a part-time job (Sodha 2017).

As long as we view workers as an unwanted expense that should be eliminated to increase profits, we will continue to increase income inequality between those who are unemployed and those who own company stock. I propose an *automation profits tax* that is based on the ratio of profits to the number of employees. Companies that employ many people like trucking companies would not be taxed, but if they laid off workers to increase profits, about half of those profits would be diverted from corporate profits into a fund that pays a basic income.

To avoid some of the opposition to giving money to people for nothing, I propose linking the idea of universal income with service to the country. I also think that everyone should file a federal tax return and pay some amount of tax to give them a sense of ownership in the country and a voice in how its money is spent (see #Tax-Return Voting).

I propose that in addition to the other measures described in this chapter, we provide a basic income guarantee to all citizens who complete two years of national service regardless of whether they earn additional money from a job (see #Create a Culture of Service and Higher Education). This income would be subject to an income tax of 5 percent, and recipients would be required to submit a federal income tax return. The amount of money each person receives would be based on the amount generated by the automation profits tax.

Job Sharing and Increased Vacation Time

The United States is the only developed country without a single legally required paid vacation day or holiday. The average private sector worker in the United States has sixteen days off, and one in four Americans does not have a single paid day off. In contrast, all the countries in the European Union (EU) have at least four weeks paid vacation (twenty days), and sixteen developed countries have twenty-five or more (Reay, Sanes and Schmitt 2013).

The United States is the only developed country that does not require employers to grant paid maternity or parental leave. The EU requires its members to grant fourteen weeks of maternity leave, and several of its members offer more (Sahadi 2016).

Despite having fewer days off than Europeans, Americans don't take all the days they can. Fifty-nine percent of US managers do not take all their vacation days, and only 39 percent of nonmanagers felt support for taking time off. One of the most common reasons cited by managers for not taking time off was that their work accumulated while they were gone. Others pointed out that their work just piled up while they were gone because no one was assigned to do the work in their absence (The High Price of Silence: Analyzing the Business Implications of an Under-vacationed Workforce 2016).

Another way to share the wealth of automation is to give employees more time off or to share jobs. Having workers spend less time on the job and more time taking vacations increases spending on tourism—jobs that cannot be exported. A report on vacations conducted by Oxford Economics concludes:

> *Vacation has the power to give American companies a competitive advantage, but only if they use it. Managers from the C-suite down need to shake free of guilt and perception issues and embrace the potential time off holds for themselves and their employees. Ignoring vacation is a choice—a choice to fall behind companies*

It also increases the opportunity for job sharing if the barrier of pretax benefits is removed.

The concept of a paid vacation day is a fiction. If the company is paying someone who is not working, either they will pressure that person to skip his or her vacations or they will save all their work for the person to catch up on when he or she returns, thus defeating the goal of relaxing and returning to work refreshed. Pay should be directly linked to the number of days worked, and when employees work less than five days a week, fifty-two weeks a year, the pay they don't receive is available to pay someone else to fill in but at the full daily wage.

I propose that we rethink the role of retirees and of vacation in terms of two-month increments where a "full-time" job is ten months a year. Two people could share a job where each of them works six months or older workers could scale back in stages to fill in for vacationing workers before full retirement. The adults would work ten months or 217 days and the school year would be increased from 180 days to 217 to match it (see #Extend the School Day to Match Parent's Workday). Families could take extended vacations at the same time, greatly enriching the tourism industry. It isn't the future the writers of the Jetsons envisioned, but it is a model that can be adapted to the future that automation is creating.

Job Sharing and Increased Vacation Time

Chapter Seven

Reorganize Health Care

This is one of the most complicated, expensive, and emotionally charged issues facing our country today. About one in four tax dollars is spent on health care. Health-insurance premiums cost another $18,000 per family divided between employers ($13,000) and workers ($5,000) (Health Insurance: Premiums and Increases 2017).

It is hard to comprehend how much of our economic productivity is spent on health care. We spend 17.6 percent of the total value of the goods and services produced in this country (GDP) on health care. For comparison, the rest of the federal budget, not counting health care, is about 15 percent of GDP (Federal Spending: Where Does the Money Go 2016).

About 9 percent of Americans do not have health insurance (Rovner 2016). The developed countries of Europe provide health care for all their citizens for less than 12 percent of their GDP (Klein 2013). Like most problems, it is also an opportunity. If we can provide quality health care for all our citizens as efficiently as countries like France, Canada, and the United Kingdom, we can use the difference to provide other services and to reduce the burden on US businesses. In this chapter, we consider proposals to change the way we do things within our present system and why it might be necessary to make a major change.

Terms and Definitions

It is particularly difficult to have productive discourse on a topic if we do not share a common vocabulary. Let's begin by defining some terms that we can use.

Medical Insurance and Health Care

We need to be clear about the term *insurance*. For the purposes of this discussion, *insurance* means *providing a guarantee against a loss* (Definition of Insurance 2017). Generally, we spread the risk of a large loss among many people—most of whom never incur such a loss—to make the insurance affordable.

Consider fire insurance. Most of us will not have to replace a house that has burned down, but it would be financially ruinous if we did, so paying for fire insurance makes sense. Companies that sell fire insurance provide a guarantee against a large loss or expense for a fee. The maximum payout is determined in advance to pay off the mortgage, replace the house, or pay a specific amount. If the company intends to make a profit, the sum of the fees must exceed the sum of the amounts paid out to cover losses. If managers in a fire-insurance company are evaluated on how great this difference is, they are motivated to either increase fees or decrease the payouts.

One way to decrease payouts for fire insurance is to screen the customers to eliminate factors that are likely to cause house fires such as smoking cigarettes in the house. The company could charge a higher fee for fire insurance if the customer is a smoker, or they could simply refuse to take them on as a client to reduce the chance of a payout. For example, when I bought an old stone farmhouse that was built in 1836, my insurance company informed me that they did not insure houses that were more than one hundred years old. I had to find a different insurance company to handle my fire insurance. A more acceptable approach is to set the base rate high and then offer discounts to homeowners who are lower risk like nonsmokers or those who take precautions like installing a fire alarm that alerts the local fire station automatically.

People who think their risk of a fire is low and don't want to pay the insurance premium do not have that choice if they bought the house with borrowed money and have a mortgage. The lender usually mandates that the home buyer pays for fire insurance to protect his or her loan. This mandate increases the number of homes that are insured, including new ones, which spreads the risk and lowers the individual payment.

The fee for insurance may be reduced by assuming some of the risk at the low end by having a deductible. For example, if you think you could handle a loss of $5,000 yourself from your savings account, you could set your deductible at $5,000 in exchange for a lower rate than if your deductible were smaller.

A fundamental factor of insurance is ignorance. None of us knows if their house will be one of the few that burn down, which is why we buy insurance and why companies issue policies to people who eventually have claims. If we knew in advance which houses would burn, the fire-insurance business would be obsolete.

In summary, the basic features of fire insurance are as follows:

- The insurance provides guarantee against a loss that is more than the insured can afford.
- Most people in the insured group will not have a large loss.
- The maximum payout is known in advance.
- Participation by most homeowners is mandated by the mortgage lenders.
- The premiums can be adjusted based on lifestyle or other factors.
- The insured can reduce premiums by taking on some of the risk for affordable losses.
- The gross profit of the company is the difference between the premiums collected and the losses covered.
- We don't know who will need it.

Medical insurance is similar to fire insurance in some ways but very different in others. Like fire insurance, medical insurance can be used to pay for unexpected, large expenses where the risk of any one of us incurring a large expense is relatively low. For example, friends of ours gave birth to a daughter who had major abnormalities in the formation of her heart and lungs. This girl had more than a dozen surgeries in the first three years of her life that cost millions of dollars. Fortunately, the surgeries have worked, and she is enjoying a normal life. Unlike fire insurance where the potential payout is limited to the cost of replacing the building, medical procedures like those provided to our friends can be unpredictably high, which is very problematic for establishing payment rates and predicting profits.

Consider the similarities and differences point-by-point (medical in italics):

- Guarantee against a loss that is more than the insured can afford—*same*.
- Most people in the insured group will not have a large loss—*the average American will have 9.2 surgeries per lifetime* (Lee, Regenbogen and Gawande 2008).
- The maximum payout is known in advance—*unknown*.
- Participation by most homeowners is mandated by the mortgage lenders—*mandated by the Affordable Care Act* (If You Don't Have Health Insurance: How Much You'll Pay 2017).
- The premiums can be adjusted based on lifestyle or other factors—*same*.
- The insured can reduce premiums by taking on some of the risk for affordable losses—*same*.
- The gross profit of the company is the difference between the premiums collected and the losses covered—*same*.
- We don't know who will need it—*changing rapidly with advances in DNA analysis* (Reilly 2012) *and DNA analysis* (Priori 2014).

For the purposes of this discussion, the term *medical insurance* describes a guarantee against an unusually large medical expense that does not happen frequently and is distinctly different from a plan to provide frequent health care.

Health care may be defined as *procedures or methods used to maintain or restore the health of the body or mind* (Healthcare n.d.). This is a very broad definition, and the problem of providing health care is complex.

Types of Health Care

One of the best problem-solving techniques I was taught as an undergraduate physics major is to take a complex problem and divide it into solvable parts. I think this is particularly important for health care because the solutions and methods of payment for each type of problem might be specific to that problem.

I propose that we define six categories of health care that may be used in following sections:

- **Prevention**: We all know that it is usually cheaper and less disruptive to prevent a problem than it is to deal with one unexpectedly. This category includes prenatal care, dental cleaning, eye checkups, nutrition education, vaccinations, and fertility control.

- **Acute care**: Health problems that arise suddenly and must have treatment immediately are acute problems. They include injuries from accidents, infections, toothaches, brain hemorrhages, heart attacks, and psychotic breaks.

- **Disability and chronic condition care**: Health problems that persist over a longer period are chronic conditions. They include physical impairment such as paralysis or loss of vision and health problems such as diabetes, anemia, arthritis, ADHD, and depression.

- **Major acute surgery**: Major acute surgery consists of operating on the body—usually the internal parts—and it is accompanied by tests, scans, and intensive care before and after the event. For the purposes of this discussion, this category will be limited to procedures that are responses to injuries, failure of necessary bodily functions, and cancer.

- **Elective surgery**: Elective surgery—for the purposes of this discussion—describes operations that are not necessary for continued survival. The category is broad. It ranges from surgery performed to improve personal appearance such as eye-lifts to hip and knee replacements to reduce pain and improve mobility. The common characteristic in this category is that the surgery does not have to be done immediately.

- **End-of-life care:** This is another broad category that is characterized by the recipient's diminished capacity to care for themselves. Examples are transportation aids, nursing, food preparation, drug administration, and physical therapy.

The following sections use the terms identified above, which may be different than those in common use. Specifically, the term *health insurance* is commonly used to describe plans that pay for health care, including extraordinary expenses. In this discussion, *health insurance* is used to describe the part of a plan that pays for large, infrequent expenses.

Electronic Medical Records

Technology can be very useful at supporting decision making and speeding up routine tasks, but it must be used within a larger strategic plan to accomplish those goals.

When I was a freshman at the University of Michigan (UM) in 1965, the university had only one computer, and I shared it with the faculty, staff, and thirty-five thousand of my fellow students. I was in line that fall for the first effort at registering for classes using computer punch cards. We collected a punch card for each class and then handed the cards to a clerk. How hard could that be? The line for registration wound around inside a gymnasium and then out the door across the main campus for three blocks. The lesson I learned that day was that computers must be matched to the system correctly to improve performance.

Computers are very good at storing and retrieving information using identification codes. For example, if you log on to Amazon.com, it will use your customer ID number to quickly retrieve a record of your past purchases and track the progress of undelivered items in a matter of seconds. To make this possible, the information must be stored in very specific ways using codes for each type of information that make the data easy to search and retrieve. Amazon does not share this information, its codes, or searching techniques with eBay or other online competitors because it wants to make it easier for you to place your next order with them than with someone else. The lesson to take away from this anecdote is that just because records are kept electronically on computers, it does not mean that the records can be easily exchanged and that private companies usually place their own interests ahead of the society at large.

A few years ago, my wife and I used to walk every morning before work with a neighbor who was the CFO at a large medical facility. I was excited about the implementation of the Health Information Technology for Economic and Clinical Health (HITECH) Act of 2009 that would replace our antiquated paper medical records with an electronic system (HITECH Act 2014). I said to her that I looked forward to the day when I could download all my medical records on to my own flash drive and take it with me on vacation to other parts of the country or I could switch to a different hospital group in my area and take all my medical records with me.

She informed me that contrary to my expectations, the new law did not require that the electronic medical records systems talk to each other. In her experience, the opposite was true. Companies that were selling electronic medical records systems were intentionally making them incompatible with each other. She pointed out that once a large hospital system adopted one of these record-keeping systems, they were locked in to that vendor because changing would be too expensive, and the vendor could charge almost any annual fee.

Seven years after HITECH, a survey of fifty-seven physicians in four states showed that they spend more than a quarter of their time on electronic health records (HER) and administrative paperwork:

> *During the office day, physicians spent 27.0% of their total time on direct clinical face time with patients and 49.2% of their time on EHR and desk work. While in the examination room with patients, physicians spent 52.9% of the time on direct clinical face time and 37.0% on EHR and desk work. The 21 physicians who completed after-hours diaries reported 1 to 2 hours of after-hours work each night, devoted mostly to EHR tasks. (Sinskey, et al. 2016)*

I propose that we revise the 2009 HITECH law to require medical records systems to communicate with each other. The intent of this proposal is to create more competition between providers and to lower the barrier to entry for new companies with better ideas so they can improve the efficiency of the doctor's time.

HIPAA

Near the end of his life, I moved my aging father from a retirement home in another state to a home near me so I could assist in his care. I discussed the issue of medical records with his doctor who had an interesting perspective. He informed me that his biggest obstacle to electronic medical record keeping was keeping the information secure. He said that the penalties for leaking confidential medical records under the Health Insurance Portability and Accountability Act of 1966 could be $50,000 per record and if someone hacked into their system and stole hundreds of records, it would bankrupt his practice (HIPAA Violations & Enforcement n.d.). He pointed to the computer in the corner of his office and told me that it was not connected to the Internet or to a wireless network.

There are many reasons that people want to keep their medical history private. One of them is that they fear that a condition that might be expensive to treat would prevent them from being hired by a firm that had to pay for their health care or be denied coverage by a health-insurance company. This fear creates a barrier that would not be necessary if health care were provided to everyone who has served his or her country (see #Create a Culture of Service and Higher Education).

I propose that we revise the HIPAA laws to allow more portability of data between medical records systems and remove the fear of losing health-care coverage if a provider or future employer finds out about a medical condition (see Health-Care Options and a Challenge).

Billing Codes

Computers work well with codes, but they can be a source of confusion when people have to provide the codes. The American Medical Association (AMA) developed the Current Procedural

Terminology (CPT) codes that describe services. For example, the CPT code for an office visit by a new patient is 99203 and 36415 is a blood draw. If a bill has a CPT code, you can look up its meaning online. The AMA does not share this list with the public, but you can look up a limited number of meanings and the amount allocated for Medicare payments if you already know the codes (CPT Code / Relative Value Search n.d.).

Insurance companies use the Healthcare Common Procedure Coding System (HCPCS). The HCPCS Level I codes are the same as the CPT codes. The HCPCS Level II codes identify products, supplies, and services. For example, E0605 is a vaporizer and L4386 is a walking splint (HCPCS 2013 Index 2013).

The World Health Organization (WHO) uses the International Classification of Diseases (ICD) to code a diagnosis. For example, a diagnosis of a sprained ankle is S93.4 (ICD-10 Version:2016 2016).

A doctor's office or hospital must assign the appropriate procedure code (CPT or HCPS Level I) with the HCPS Level II code for any service, product, or supplies and the ICD code for the diagnosis. Assignment of the correct code is usually done manually by an office worker who already knows most of the common codes or who must use his or her judgment to determine which code best describes the three parts of the service event. There is an obvious opportunity for human error while entering three or more codes per bill.

One of the men I know used to work for an insurance company as a computer programmer. His job was to write programs that would reject claims for payment. Part of the job was to catch errors. For example, if someone was treated for a sprained ankle (ICD code S93.4) and the code was entered incorrectly as S90.4 (a jaw injury), the program would automatically deny the request for reimbursement of an ankle X-ray and an ankle splint. He went on to explain that another of his tasks was to compare the doctor's diagnosis with similar diagnoses for which the payment was less and automatically change the claim code (Bihari 2016). It is important to remember that for-profit health-insurance companies make more money if they pay less.

Expert Computer Systems

If you have ever used a tax-preparation software like TurboTax, you are familiar with an expert computer system. You fill out forms and respond to questions, and then the expert system determines which tax laws apply, recommends the lowest cost options, and calculates the tax you owe or how much refund you will get. Perhaps you've heard of Watson—the IBM expert system that won the Jeopardy challenge in 2011. In that game, it was demonstrated that a computer could draw on a large database of factual information and retrieve the most likely correct answer faster than the best humans (Best 2016). Because computers double in power (or shrink in size and cost) by a factor of two every two years, the computer that ran the Watson program in 2011 is one-eighth of its former cost/size in 2017 and will continue to become more affordable for everyday use (Newcomb 2016).

Medical research is discovering new treatments daily, and new drugs are being created that have side effects and interactions with other drugs. This is more information than a single person can assimilate. Doctors need expert help to take advantage of the latest discoveries and to avoid negative outcomes due to allergic reactions or unwanted interactions with other drugs.

An expert system like Watson, programmed with medical decisions, coupled with a database of patient history, the research published in the world's medical journals, and drug interactions, could provide a major breakthrough in improving the quality of health care while simultaneously reducing the cost (Spear 2016).

Medical Paralegal

The legal profession deals with a large body of case law by employing paralegal staff who spend time with electronic search software like Westlaw locating legal precedents that might relate to a case (Thomson Reuters Westlaw n.d.). A similar position could be created in health care. A paramedical person could be trained to gather information from patients, take digital photos of visible conditions, and enter this information into a medical expert system.

I propose that we provide everyone with access to the results of the latest medical research and the accumulated knowledge of the best doctors by using an expert system like IBM's Watson combined with paramedical staff. Diagnosis and recommendations for medical treatment would be reviewed first by the paramedical person and the patient. Either of these people could request that a doctor review the data and the diagnosis to catch computer errors. In addition to recommending which tests have to be done and a course of treatment, the expert system could also inform the patient of the price and availability of services, supplies, and treatment facilities.

Prevention and Acute Care for Everyone

We build fire stations in our neighborhoods because we acknowledge the wisdom of stopping fires before they spread, regardless of where the fires start, and by enforcing electrical building codes to prevent many fires from occurring. Similarly, it makes sense to stop the spread of disease by treating anyone who displays symptoms and by doing what we can to prevent disease. We are also compassionate people, and it is not in most of our natures to turn away the sick and injured because they are poor.

Koop on Prevention

One of our country's most influential figures was C. Everett Koop who was appointed surgeon general by President Reagan. Koop strongly opposed abortion and recognized that agreement on the topic of abortion was unlikely. Instead, he advocated better sex education and the use of five-year hormone implants to prevent unintended pregnancy (Dr. Koop's Abortion Advice 1989).

Initially, Democrats opposed his appointment because he testified that he had never seen a situation where the mother's life was endangered by a pregnancy that couldn't be resolved by a cesarean birth and that he was strongly opposed to abortion. Neither Republicans nor Democrats were prepared for what they got— someone who followed the facts and the science. When asked by the

Republicans to testify that having an abortion caused harm to the mother, after examining the evidence, he responded that the evidence did not support such a conclusion.

Dr. Koop enraged his most ardent supporter—Republican Senator Jesse Helms from North Carolina—when he came out strongly against smoking and being around smokers. He is the "surgeon general" who put the warning on today's cigarette packages. Here are some of his thoughts on smoking:

> *Cigarette smoking is clearly identified as the chief, preventable cause of death in our society.*
>
> *A thousand people will stop smoking today. Their funerals will be held sometime in the next three or four days.*
>
> *The right of smokers to smoke ends where their behavior affects the health and well-being of others.* (Koop n.d.b)

Dr. Koop also shocked the religious right when he publicly advocated sex education as part of the campaign against the spread of HIV/AIDS. In 1988, he mailed a brochure to every American household describing the types of risky behaviors that could spread the HIV virus and advocated the use and distribution of condoms (Koop, The C. Everett Koop Papers n.d.).

Dr. Koop expanded the role of the surgeon general's office to include issues of family health, and he encouraged prenatal care, preschool education, and childhood fitness. More examples of Dr. Koop's ideas are as follows:

> *The target audience goes back to conception. That means pre-natal care, safe delivery, post-natal screening, and the ordinary stuff you do in pediatrics.*
>
> *Your choice of diet can influence your long term health prospects more than any other action you might take.*

When a child shows up for school, and is not physically and mentally ready to learn, he or she never catches up.

If you have a kid who goes to kindergarten and doesn't know what a circle is, doesn't know what red and green are, and doesn't know what right and left are, by the time he learns those things, the rest of the class is far ahead of him.

Risks I think are the thing that make life important and everything that you and I do is risk vs. benefit. Is there a risk to sending your kid out? Absolutely. Is there a benefit? It exceeds the risk.

Make your kids go out and play. Kids ought to grow up the way you and I grew up and we grew up fifty years apart or maybe more. But we did the same things. Now who's out playing in the afternoon? Nobody.

Dr. Koop was an ardent opponent of abortion, but he did not use his office to further his personal belief. Instead, he sought to respect each other's rights:

The American ideal is not that we all agree with each other, or even like each other, every minute of the day. It is rather that we will respect each other's rights, especially the right to be different, and that, at the end of the day, we will understand that we are one people, one country, and one community, and that our well-being is inextricably bound up with the well-being of each and every one of our fellow citizens. (Koop, C. Everett Koop Quotes and Sayings n.d.)

Because each of us benefits from the well-being of all of us, I propose that we provide prevention—including hormone-based fertility control—and acute care services to everyone at no charge using a combination of paramedical people and expert computer systems.

Disability, Wheelchairs, and New Technology
When I was in my twenties, I talked to an insurance agent, and one of the topics we talked about was disability insurance. My thought

was that if I were partially disabled, I would want to be able to buy whatever technology I needed to restore my ability to work and live a normal life. For example, if I lost the use of my legs, I would explore buying a high-tech chair that could stand up, climb stairs, and use existing bathroom facilities and replace my car with a lift van. To that end, I would want an insurance policy that had an up-front payout but no long-term benefit. I was told at that time that the only way I could get a payout like that would be if I were injured in an auto accident because auto-accident insurance was the only type that had a large settlement payout. He said I could get long-term disability insurance that paid a percentage of my present salary but that had no big, up-front cash payout.

Forty years later, we seem to be stuck in a time warp. Instead of providing people the latest personal transportation vehicles, we have renovated our buildings to accommodate the limitations of one-hundred-year-old technology—the wheelchair. The wheelchair has been around since 1595 and has remained essentially unchanged for the last one hundred years (Bellis n.d.).

There are several mobility solutions today that are better than the wheelchair. Examples include the Tec RMD for use indoors and the Toyota iBot from the inventor of the Segway for multiterrain travel (New Divice Makes Wheelchairs Obsolete 2012); (Toyota iBOT Wheelchair 2016).

I propose that we change our Medicare, Medicaid, and insurance rules to focus on using the best technology available to address disability issues, especially in mobility and communications. The role of government agencies would be to certify technologies to determine if they meet reliability and safety standards and that they live up to their claims but let the individual choose. This would invigorate innovators and let the market reward the best devices.

End-of-Life Health Care

About five years ago when my father was ninety-eight, he was diagnosed with a recurrence of bowel cancer. I was told that if we didn't operate, he would die painfully within days but if we did operate, he might never fully recover but it would put off his death for the time being. Because he was suffering from mild dementia, the decision was up to me. He had the operation, and, as predicted, he did not fully recover. He was plagued by itchy skin that we couldn't cure, so he was uncomfortable all the time. One nurse told me that itchy skin might be a referred pain from his bowel operation, so treating his skin with lotion wasn't likely to alleviate his discomfort.

As his health deteriorated, he needed constant nursing. His bill at the nursing home toward the end was $10,000 a month. Even though he had adequate medical insurance for the operations and doctor care, he was spending his life savings on nursing care at a rate that would exhaust it within a few months, and he was miserable. His doctor would not declare that he was likely to die within a few months, so his medical insurance wouldn't pay for hospice. We switched doctors to one that the hospice people recommended who determined that my father was likely to die soon, so he would qualify. Once on hospice, they would give him morphine to make him more comfortable, but they had to increase the dose to remain effective. One day, the nurse told me that an increased dose might be fatal, but it was the only option for giving him enough relief so that he could sleep. I told them to do what was necessary to make him comfortable. He died in his sleep that night.

I vowed that when my time came, I would not put my children in the position I was in and I would try to preserve as much of my life savings for their benefit as I could. Living another few months in misery was not what I wanted.

Later, I found out that my father's experience was not unusual. About eight out of ten people who die each year in the United States are on Medicare. Medicare reports that about 25 percent of the amount spent on senior adults over the age of sixty-five occurs in the last year of life. In their last year of life, they were being treated for a variety of diseases concurrently at a substantially higher rate than other Medicare recipients:

- hypertension (67 percent);

- ischemic heart disease (53 percent);
- chronic kidney disease (51 percent);
- congestive heart failure (48 percent);
- Alzheimer's disease or dementia (43 percent);
- diabetes (38 percent); and
- cancer (17 percent).

The United States is changing the way it deals with end-of-life care by utilizing hospice and allowing people to die at home rather than in hospitals which costs less.

I propose that we adopt the same model of care at the end of life used by European countries that emphasized home hospice care rather than hospital care that limits the money spent on surgeries near the end of life but that the change would be phased in over an eight-year period (End-of-Life Care in Canada More Hospital-Centric than in U.S., Europe 2016). The intent of the phase-in period would be to allow those who want to have extra surgeries near the end of their lives to buy supplementary insurance.

History of Taxes and Health Benefits

Our attitudes toward health-care benefits and taxes on those benefits developed over almost the whole history of our country. Here are some historical highlights to provide perspective on this issue (emphasis added):

> *1789—Congress establishes the U.S. Marine Hospital Service. The service was funded by compulsory contributions from seamen's wages.*

> *1847—The Massachusetts Health Insurance Company of Boston becomes the first insurer to issue sickness insurance.*

> *1849—New York passes the first general insurance law.*

1853—French mutual aid society, La Societe Francaise de Bienfaisance Mutuelle, establishes prepaid hospital care plan in San Francisco.

1863—The Travelers Insurance Company of Hartford, CT, offers accident insurance for railway mishaps (followed by other forms of accident insurance). Travelers was the first to issue insurance resembling today's policies.

1870s—Railroad, mining, and other industries begin to provide company doctors funded by deductions from workers' wages.

1877—Granite Cutters Union establishes first national sick benefit program.

1910—Montgomery Ward & Co. enters into one of the earliest group insurance contracts.

1913—International Ladies Garment Workers Union (ILGWU) begins first union medical services.

1915-1920s—Efforts to establish compulsory health insurance programs fail in 16 states.

1929—A group of schoolteachers arranges for Baylor Hospital in Dallas, TX, to provide room, board, and specified services at a predetermined monthly cost. This plan is considered the forerunner of Blue Cross plans.

1937—Blue Cross Commission established.

1939—Revenue Act of 1939 (Sec. 104), establishes employee tax exclusion for compensation for injuries, sickness, or both received under workers' compensation, accident, or health insurance.

1949—Supreme Court upholds National Labor Relations Board ruling that employee benefits are subject to collective bargaining.

1954—Revenue Act of 1954 (Sec. 106) excludes from taxation employers' contributions to accident and health plans benefiting employees, and clarifies that such contributions had always been deductible as business expenses.

1965—Medicare and Medicaid legislation passed as Title XVIII and Title XIX of the Social Security Act.

1968—Firestone Tire and Rubber Co. begins to self-fund health benefits.

1973—Health Maintenance Organization (HMO) Act of 1973 establishes benefit, administrative, financial, and contractual requirements for entities seeking designation as federally qualified HMOs. The act also requires most employers who offer an HMO to offer a federally qualified HMO.

1974—Employee Retirement Income Security Act of 1974 (ERISA) establishes uniform standards that employee benefit plans must follow to obtain and maintain their tax-favored status. ERISA supersedes or preempts all state law otherwise applicable to pension and welfare plans covered by ERISA. ERISA still recognizes the states' role in regulating insurance.

1978—Pregnancy Discrimination Act amends Title VII of the Civil Rights Act of 1964. Requires that employers treat disabilities and medical conditions associated with pregnancy and childbirth the same as other disabilities or medical conditions.

1984—Deficit Reduction Act of 1984 (DEFRA) changes the tax treatment and contribution limits of voluntary employee beneficiary associations (VEBAs) and imposes new nondiscrimination rules for VEBAs similar to those for tax-qualified pension and profit-sharing plans. DEFRA makes Medicare the secondary payer for covered health expenses of workers ages 65-69 who are covered by an employer plan.

1986—Consolidated Omnibus Budget Reconciliation Act of 1985 (COBRA) requires employers with 20 or more employees to offer continued health coverage to terminated employees and dependents for a specified period (18 or 36 months).

1996—Health Insurance Portability and Accountability Act of 1996 (HIPAA) sets national nondiscrimination and "portability" standards for individual health insurance coverage, HMOs, and group health plans; establishes tax-favored treatment of long-term care insurance. The administrative simplification section of the act calls for regulations on standard electronic formats and for the privacy of personal health information. The act institutes a pilot medical savings account (MSA) program, limited to 750,000 individuals by the year 2000. See Consolidated Appropriations Act of 2001, enacted in 2000, for extension of MSA pilot program.

1997—Balanced Budget Act of 1997 (BBA) provides several health benefits related provisions. Creates Medicare+Choice program. Establishes new guarantee opportunities for Medicare supplement policies in conjunction with the expansion of private plan options. Creates the Children's Health Insurance Program (CHIP), a new state children's health program, modifies Medicaid to increase state flexibility in administering the program, and provides $24 billion in federal funds over five years to support the program.

1998—Omnibus Consolidated and Emergency Supplemental Appropriations Act requires plans to provide coverage for reconstructive surgery after mastectomies.

2000—Electronic Signatures in Global and National Commerce Act of 2000 gives electronic signatures and records the same weight as written signatures and records, which should lead to easier administration of

> *electronic benefit, compensation, and human resources
> systems. (History of Health Insurance Benefits 2002)*

This history shows some interesting characteristics, which are as follows:

- As early as 1789, Congress decided that payment of health-insurance premiums must be required to get full compliance.
- In the 1870s, companies provided health services at employee expense.
- In 1939, the government recognized that company money spent on employee health care should be considered a business expense and not taxed.
- In 1949, the Supreme court ruled that employee benefits are subject to collective bargaining.

It makes sense that if a company spends part of its profits on providing health care and it is a part of an employee's compensation package, it should be able to deduct that money from its profits and therefore not have to pay taxes on that money. Unfortunately, this reasoning led to some unintended consequences:

- The employer became the customer of the health-insurance companies rather than the person who is receiving the service.
- The price of a procedure is hidden from the consumer of the service and is not considered by those who have health insurance.
- Hidden prices result in widely varying charges for the same procedures by factors up to one hundred (Young and Kirkham 2013).
- People are frightened of losing their health-care coverage if they lose their job.
- People are afraid of losing their health-care coverage if their insurance company or employer finds out about a medical condition (see #HIPAA).
- Costs are rising at an unsustainable rate. The average is now $10,000 per person per year (Alonso-Zaldivar 2016).

The present system must be changed. The question is how to change it.

Health-Care Options and a Challenge

When we talk about the cost of health care, we cannot escape the fact that we pay more in the United States for the same treatments than other countries pay. Comparisons are difficult because countries with a central health-care system set prices, while in the United States, the cost can vary depending on whether the customer is a big health-care plan or a private individual.

On May 4, 2017, after a republican health bill had passed the House, President Trump said to the president of Australia, "It's going to be fantastic health care. I shouldn't say this to our great gentleman and my friend from Australia because you have better health care than we do" (Westcott 2017) Australia has a universal health-care system paid for by the government that is very different from the plan approved by the House, but the President is correct that it covers more people and costs less than health care in the United States. Here are some comparisons between the United States and Australia for health care in US dollars. The two costs shown for the United States are the average and the top 5 percent:

- Cost per hospital day: US $4,287 (average), $12,537 (top 5 percent) versus Aus. $1,472
- Angioplasty: US $28,182, $61,649 versus Aus. $8,911
- Bypass: US $73,420, $150,515 versus Aus. $43,230
- Hip replacement: US $40,364, $87,987 versus Aus. $27,810
- Normal birth: US $9,775, $16,653 versus Aus. $6,846
- Appendectomy: US $13,851, $29,426 versus Aus. $5,467

We also pay much more for the same drugs. Here are comparisons between the United States and the United Kingdom (UK). The first two figures for the United States are the average and top 5 percent:

- Nexium: US $202 (average), $373 (top 5 percent) versus UK $32
- Lipitor: US $124, $145 versus UK $43

- Celebrex: US $162, $258 versus UK $116

Australia spends 9.1 percent of its gross domestic product (GDP) on health, the United Kingdom spends 9.6 percent, while the United States spends 17.6 percent (Klein 2013).

Critics of government health-care programs cite poor service and long waits to receive treatment. A study by the Commonwealth Fund found these comparisons between the United States and Australia (Osborn and Schoen 2013). Those comparisons that are favorable to the United States are enhanced.

- Same-day or next-day appointment when sick: Australian 58 percent versus US 48 percent
- Waited six days or more to an appointment: Australian 14 percent versus US 26 percent
- After-hours care without emergency room visit: Australian 46 percent versus US 39 percent
- Used emergency room in the past two years: Australian 22 percent versus US uninsured 48 percent
- *Wait times for specialist appointment less than four weeks: Australian 51 percent versus US 76 percent*

Some people are convinced that private enterprise can do everything better than the government. Clearly, this is not the case when we compare our system with those of other developed countries where the government provides health care for all citizens.

I've made some suggestions that would be compatible with private health-care providers, but it remains to be seen if private health-care providers are motivated enough to make major changes that would reduce their income.

I see three options for revising our health-care system:

- Competitive Health Care (CHC) paid for by the patient who may shop independently for best price and service or join co-ops that bid for packages of services

- Government Regulated Monopolies (GRM) like electric utilities
- Government Health Care (GHC) system like those in the United Kingdom, France, and Canada

Competitive Health Care (CHC)

The present system is a patchwork of practices that have developed historically and need to be revised if they are to be affordable. The cost of services is often disconnected from the patient so that market forces do not restrain prices. For example, my doctor suggested that I get a MRI (magnetic resonance image). When I went to schedule the procedure, they asked if I had ever experienced claustrophobia during a previous MRI. I had a mild experience one time out of four previous visits, so I told her that yes, I had. She suggested that I use a newer model machine that had a larger opening. I asked if it cost more, but she had no idea. I got the usual answer: "Your insurance will pay for it." I was willing to put up with some mild discomfort if the difference in cost was a thousand dollars even if I didn't have to pay for it directly for the good of the system, but I didn't have enough information to make the decision.

Many PHC providers are trying to keep the cost of their health-care plans down by increasing the deductible. In 2016, more than half of the private health plans had deductibles of more than $1,000 (More Workers Enroll in High Deductible Plans... 2016). This practice does create some incentive to shop for price on treatments and procedures that are less than the deductible, but it is still difficult. To compare prices, you must be sure to compare prices for the same procedure that is indicated by its CPT code (see #Billing Codes). The cost of an MRI can vary dramatically by state and by the type of facility providing the service. For example, in Michigan where I live most of the year, the cost of an MRI can vary from as little as $500 at an imaging center up to $2,900 at a hospital (Ramsey 2017).

Simply increasing the deductible is a stopgap measure that only introduces market forces on prices that total less than the patient's deductible.

Government Regulated Monopoly (GRM)

A monopoly is a situation where one company controls the prices and supply in a particular sector of the economy or geographical region. In most cases, the government acts to prevent the creation of monopolies in the public interest to keep prices low by assuring that there is competition. In some instances, the economy of scale is so great that a single large provider of a good or service can have the best price. An electric utility is a good example of a regulated, large-scale monopoly. It would be very wasteful to have two or three sets of electric lines running to each neighborhood in competition with each other. Where this is the case, a company is allowed to have a monopoly, but their prices and profits are regulated by a government body.

A regulated monopoly in health care might be a good option in sparsely populated areas where there are too few people to support more than one treatment facility or for very expensive high-tech equipment like an ion accelerator used for proton-radiation treatment.

Proton-beam therapy has the potential to kill cancer tumors more effectively than radiation treatment that uses photons of light in the X-ray or gamma ray energy range. A beam of protons consists of positively charged particles that deliver most of the beam's energy near the end of its path. The length of the path through tissue depends on the initial speed of the particles that can be controlled in the ion accelerator. The beam can be steered by magnets to "paint" irregularly shaped tumors. These characteristics might make a proton beam irradiation treatment a better choice for treating cancers near other critical organs like the eye or brain.

The problem is that these systems cost about $40 million. Leading hospitals compete for top doctors who are interested in conducting research using the latest and greatest technology, and to maintain their reputation as one of the best, there is pressure to buy one of these systems rather than send patients to another hospital. This attitude is demonstrated by a recent press release from a hospital in Detroit, Michigan:

                    Health-Care Options and a Challenge

Beaumont's center is one of just 25 operational proton therapy centers in the U.S.

"This means that cancer patients from other states and countries will travel to Michigan for proton therapy, making Beaumont even more of a destination center for cancer care," said Dr. Stevens. (Beaumont Health First in Michigan to Treat Cancer Patient with Protons 2017)

Most aspects of health care, in my opinion, are not a good match for GRM, but it might play a role for specific situations due to low population density or very expensive, new equipment.

Government Health Care (GHC)

This approach is an anathema to many conservatives, but it is worthwhile to consider an existing government health-care program that most conservatives support—the Veterans Administration (VA).

The Veterans Administration

The VA operated 144 hospitals and served 5.9 million people in 2015 (Department of Veterans Affairs Fast Facts 2016). The VA is an integrated system that controls the facilities and payment for care.

Medicare

Medicare is another government program that benefits disabled and elderly Americans. Unlike the VA, it does not control the facilities and caregivers. Instead, it pays for service from private hospitals and care providers. It influences cost by limiting the amount it will pay for each procedure or service, but providers can charge more. Medicare pays for the care of about forty-nine million citizens who are sixty-five and older and for nine million people who are disabled (CMS Fast Fact 2017).

Medicare Part A

Medicare has several parts; Part A pays for hospital expenses according to the following conditions:

Monthly Premium

> *Nothing if you or your spouse worked for 10 years or more in the U.S.*
>
> *$227 if you or your spouse worked between 7.5 and 10 years in the U.S.*
>
> *$413 if you or your spouse worked fewer than 7.5 years in the U.S.*

Inpatient Hospital Care

> *$1,316 deductible for each benefit period*
>
> *No coinsurance for days 1 to 60*
>
> *$329 daily coinsurance for days 61 to 90*
>
> *$658 daily coinsurance for 60 lifetime reserve days*

Skilled Nursing Facility Care

> *No deductible for each benefit period*
>
> *No coinsurance for days 1 to 20*
>
> *$164.50 daily coinsurance for days 21 to 100*

Home Health Care

> *No deductible or coinsurance*

Hospice Care

> *No deductible*
>
> *Small copayment for outpatient drugs and inpatient respite care*

(What Do I Have to Pay for Services Covered Under Medicare Part A? 2017)

Medicare Part B

Medicare Part B pays for health care according to the following guidelines:

Monthly Premium

> *$134 if your annual income is below $85,000 ($170,000 for couples). If you are covered by hold harmless, on average you will pay $109.*

People with high incomes have a higher Part B premium.

Annual Deductible

$183

Doctor and other medical services

20% if your provider accepts assignment2

Outpatient hospital care

Coinsurance or copayment that can be no higher than the Part A hospital deductible ($1,316 in 2017)

Home health care

Nothing

Clinical diagnostic lab services

Nothing

Other diagnostic tests and x-rays4

20%

Diabetes self-management supplies (glucose monitors, lancets, test strips)

20%

Durable medical equipment (e.g., wheelchairs, hospital beds) (see #Disability, Wheelchairs, and New Technology)

20%

Physical therapy services

20%

Ambulance services

20%

Chiropractor services

20%

Outpatient mental health services

20%

Annual Wellness Visit

> *Nothing*
>
> *Preventive Care*
>
> *You pay nothing for many preventive care services that are recommended by the U.S. Preventive Services Task Force. There may be copays and deductibles for some preventive services. (Medicare Part B costs 2017)*

Medicare Part C

Medicare Part C allows for creation of private groups such as Health Maintenance Organizations (HMOs) and Preferred Provider Organizations (PPOs) to provide the same services using different combinations of fees. These plans are called Medicare Advantage Plans.

Medicare Part D

Medicare Part D pays for prescription drugs (What Does Medicare Cover (Parts A, B, C, and D)? 2017).

Medicaid and CHIP

Medicaid and the Children's Health Insurance Program (CHIP) provide health-care coverage for about seventy-four million low-income and disabled Americans. Medicaid is a cooperative program between state and federal governments. Prior 2010, the federal government identified about sixty categories of people who qualified for Medicaid that focused on the poor, children, disabled, and pregnant women (Eligibility n.d.). The Affordable Care Act of 2010 offered states a deal to expand coverage to include all people who earned less than 133 percent of the federal poverty level in which the federal government would pay for the expanded coverage for the first three years and then for 90 percent of it after that. Thirty-one states accepted the deal, and health-care coverage was expanded to about twenty million more people, but nineteen states did not.

Health-Care Challenge

Our health care is a piecemeal approach that provides health care for about 89 percent of the population and leaves about twenty-seven

     Health-Care Options and a Challenge

million adults without health-care insurance (Who Are the Remaining Uninsured Americans? 2017). Our national focus has been on finding a way to pay for our existing system instead of radically changing that system to reduce its costs by 40 percent to match the costs paid by other countries and covering everyone.

Many people believe that our private companies and free-market system are better at any task than the government. I'd like to give those companies an opportunity to prove it.

I propose that we issue a challenge to the private health-care and insurance industry and give them seven years to prove they can provide health care at the same cost as government programs in other countries and reduce the cost of health care in the United States from 17.6 percent of GDP to just above that of most developed countries at 10.6 percent or 60 percent of the present amount.

If the private health-care companies cannot meet this challenge by achieving milestones of 1 percent of GDP reduction per year for seven years, then I propose that we replace our current system with a national health-care system (see #Paying for New Programs).

Health-Care Options and a Challenge

Chapter Eight
Adapt to Longer Life-Spans and a Graceful Exit

When I was seventeen, I traveled to Pensacola, Florida, where I experienced swimming in the ocean for the first time. While standing in the surf area, I started talking to my friend, Bob, who was closer to the shore and turned my back to the sea. Suddenly I found myself upside down with my feet out of the water and my back on the bottom being swept along by a larger-than-expected wave. Dealing with changing technology can be like swimming in the surf. If you just try to stand still with your back to what's coming, you will get pummeled. If you can see the wave coming and time your move correctly, you can have a great ride.

Aging

Scientific discoveries and their application in new technologies have made significant changes in our lives already, but bigger-than-usual waves of change might be coming in the next few years that will affect how much time and money we have in the last stage of our lives.

Social Security and Medicare trust funds accumulate money in advance of our old age to provide income after we stop earning money. The big question is "For how long?" When Social Security was created in 1935, the average life expectancy was sixty-one and the typical retirement age was sixty-five (Escamilla n.d.). Now the life expectancy is eighty-one years, but we are still retiring at about the same age. This change has been gradual and predictable. In 1983, the government increased the payroll tax to build up the Social Security fund (see #Empty Trust Funds) in anticipation of the retirement of the large number of people born shortly after the end of World War II—the baby boomers (Sanders 2015).

There are two developments in science and technology that might change life expectancy dramatically—a cure for cancer and a cure for aging. If either of these "waves" hits us when we aren't expecting them, they can completely upset our retirement system.

Cure for Cancer

The National Institutes of Health invests $32 billion annually, most of which employs three hundred thousand researchers at more than twenty-five hundred schools and institutions (Budget: Research for the People 2017). Biological science is making the same kind of difference in this century that computers did in the last one. One of the goals for this research is a cure for cancer. About six hundred thousand people die of cancer in the United States each year (Cancer Statistics 2016). In my youth, a diagnosis of cancer was a death sentence. Now, most of us know people who have recovered from cancer. One example is President Jimmy Carter whose treatment for metastatic melanoma succeeded in a remission of the cancer (Mohney 2016).

One problem with achieving this goal is that cancer is not a single disease, and a particular therapy might help with one type but not others. A new approach that holds promise for dealing with a range of cancers is to help one's own immune system fight the cancer by sensitizing it to the cancer that is present (Regalado 2015).

Cure for Aging

Another development that could disrupt our health-care system would be an effective "cure" for aging. One of the great equalizers of humanity is the certain knowledge that we are all going to die someday, and we know that very few of us will live more than a hundred years. In recent years, our thinking has changed. Some of us now consider aging as a defect that can be fixed.

In 1962, biologist Leonard Hayflick discovered that human cells replicate a limited number of times. An explanation for this limit is related to how strands of DNA—the long molecules in the cell nucleus that are the blueprints of cell function—terminate in repeating sequences called *telomeres*. You can think of these telomeres as the plastic tips on your shoelaces. Scientists have also observed that each time a cell divides, the sequence of telomeres gets shorter, and when they were gone, the cell malfunctions or dies like your shoelaces fray when the plastic tips are gone. Cancer cells have the ability to replace the telomeres and can divide without limit. Scientists are exploring the possibility of using this trait of cancer to extend the life of healthy cells (Starr 2017).

Most of our DNA exists in the nucleus of our cells, and we inherit half of it from each parent when the nucleus divides to form egg or sperm cells. A smaller amount of DNA exists outside the cell nucleus in small bodies called *mitochondria*. The mitochondria do not divide like the nucleus, and we inherit all our mitochondrial DNA from our mothers. The nucleus has repair mechanisms to fix broken or malformed DNA that are not present in the mitochondria, so changes to the DNA in the mitochondria can be passed down through the generations through the maternal line. This feature is useful in tracing human history, and it was the best proof that the bones found under a parking lot in England were those of King Richard III because the mitochondrial DNA in those bones has the same rare mutation found in living descendants of Richard's mother (Rincon 2014).

Researchers from Caltech and UCLA think that mutated and damaged mitochondrial DNA build up in cells and are the cause of age-related illness. They have discovered a treatment that might be used to periodically flush out the damaged DNA and restore the cells to full function—effectively stopping the aging process (Turning Back the Aging Clock 2016).

Retirement

For most of human history, people worked until they died at whatever task they could still manage. Emperor William I of Germany introduced the idea in 1889—at the suggestion of Otto von Bismarck—of allowing workers to retire at the age of seventy:

> *Those who are disabled from work by age and invalidity*
> *have a well-grounded claim to care from the state.*
> *(Otto von Bismarck n.d.)*

The average lifetime in Germany at that time was about seventy. Germany later lowered the retirement age to sixty-five, which served as a model for the US retirement system. When the United States adopted the retirement age of sixty-five in 1935, the life expectancy for American men was about fifty-eight (Laskow 2014). Since the end of the depression, the US life expectancy has increased to seventy-six for men and eighty-one for females, but the retirement age has not changed (Bernstein 2016).

In the 2016 election, three of the top candidates (Sanders, Trump, and Clinton) were all over the age of sixty-five, and nine of the sixteen presidential candidates would have reached the age of retirement (sixty-five) before the end of their first term, if elected (Exner 2016). This statistic indicates that many people have something to offer in the form of public service after the current age of retirement.

I propose that we reconsider the concept of retirement and allow people to phase out of the workforce in stages and choose to retire whenever they have the inclination and financial ability to do so (see #US Service Corps). A potential retiree could substitute for workers on leave or vacation and gradually reduce the number of months worked each year until full retirement (see #Job Sharing and Increased Vacation Time).

Graceful Exit

One of the unusual things about human brains is that we have the ability to imagine the future. Neuroscientists have found that we use the same parts of the brain when we imagine the future as when we remember the past (Biello 2007). This skill has proven valuable to our species by anticipating threats and making plans for times of famine or flood. Many people use this ability to imagine what comes after death, and many do not accept that our existence ends when our brains die. They believe in some form of afterlife, while some others do not.

My father lived to the age of ninety-eight, and I was with him often in the last years of his life. I watched him decline and deal with almost constant discomfort and pain until his death. I do not believe in an afterlife, and I decided at that time that I will choose the manner and time of my death if possible. I don't want to ask someone else to take on the responsibility or emotional hardship of ending my life, so I'll have to do it while I'm still able. I don't think there will be many people who make that choice, and it is important that they are not coerced.

I propose that along with legalizing and monitoring drugs like heroin, it is possible for an individual to choose to end his or her life by requesting enough heroin or other drug to cause a fatal overdose. To prevent coercion, the applicant would have to get the request approved by a judge who would determine that the person is capable of making this decision and that those who might benefit from his or her death had not coerced the person into this action. This option would also be available to those who are serving extended sentences in prisons if they do not wish to continue living (see #Reorganize Prisons).

I plan to have a dignified ceremony with family and friends to say good-bye. I call this a *graceful exit*. It isn't for those who believe differently about the afterlife, but I suggest that those who disagree with them are not prevented from ending their life in a manner of their own choosing.

Chapter Nine

Change the Priorities of Education

I've worked as a teacher for most of my career at the high-school and college levels, and I've seen many ideas come and go for fixing the system, but few, if any of them, make any difference. My favorite challenge to professional educators is the following:

> *I'm from the computer generation where the power of computers doubles every two years. What measurable outcome of the educational system has improved by a factor of two in the last one hundred years? Do students learn twice as much? Do they graduate in half the time? Does it cost half as much? Are graduates able to reason and solve problems twice as well or as fast? (Preston, 2017)*

The system hasn't been able to achieve even this modest goal because it is the wrong goal. I suggest we recognize that our schools are not factories that produce product for the next level of school or for the workforce, but rather it is a place where children spend a lot of time while they mature. The appropriate goals for our schools are to help them transition from immature children to mature adults who are equipped to handle the responsibilities of interpersonal relationships, parenting, work, and participating in community activities.

Expand the Measurements of Success and Change Focus

We've all heard a student ask why they need to take a particular class only to be told that they have to have it to get into college, and when they ask why they should go to college, the answer is to get a good job and earn more money. When fourteen-year-old children seek guidance on what educational path to choose, they are told to pick something they are passionate about when they don't know enough about the choices to have an opinion, let alone a passion.

Is it a surprise that our children feel stressed and anxious? The National Institute of Mental Health tells us that one in four children ages thirteen to eighteen have some type of anxiety disorder (Any

Anxiety Disorder among Children n.d.). This statistic is representative of my small circle of adult male friends when we talk about their children.

The first step to making our schools better is to measure and evaluate them on how well they are helping our children to mature and deal with stress. For example, we can periodically ask the following questions:

- Do you feel physically safe while you are in school?
- Do you feel that you can ask questions without being ridiculed for not knowing?
- Do you feel that your peers discourage you from excelling in your schoolwork?
- Are you being bullied either in person or online?
- Are you getting good advice from your teachers on how to develop friendships?
- Do you have one or more close friends?
- Are you getting better at listening?
- Are you comfortable with your sexual identity?
- Do you think that you are getting better at learning new ideas?
- Do you think you are getting better at distinguishing truth from lies?
- Are you excited about learning in at least one of your classes?
- Do you feel that your school is a community of which you are a part?
- Are you identifying jobs that are worth doing that you might like to try?
- Are you optimistic about your future?

Change the Role of Schools and Parents

If we change the emphasis of education from the factory model to one of helping students to mature, other forms of teaching and learning become more attractive.

Internet technologies have made it possible for everyone to watch well-designed, entertaining presentations by master teachers online. To achieve the goal of helping our students to mature into successful adults, it is time to make some basic changes to the culture of K–12 education. I propose the following changes:

Meals, Group Activity, Practice, and Introspection
When we bring students together in school buildings, we have the opportunity to involve them in group activities where they can develop social skills to help them mature. The school day should feature activities that are considered extracurricular now such as sports, music, and theater. It should also take advantage of specialized spaces and expensive equipment, so school is where students do science labs, make things in art and woodworking, and learn how to repair things in mechanics classes. Students tend to enjoy these activities and are willing to spend time doing them. Students could learn family-building skills like cooking, childcare, and elder care.

Extend the School Day to Match Parent's Workday
One of the most valuable functions of school for parents is to provide day care while they work. Because teachers and students cannot take too many hours of traditional classes, the school day and school year are limited to a shorter period than most people work, which results in the need for expensive before- and after-school care, "summer school," or unsupervised children.

I propose that the school day include breakfast and lunch and consist of a mixture of group activities, lab work, "homework," and introspection and last from about 7:30 a.m. until 5:30 p.m. Periods of introspection would give the students an opportunity for quiet time and rest while learning techniques such as yoga, meditation, or prayerfulness, which could help with reducing anxiety and depression. Students would be grouped into "families" of twelve students, including students of all ages that would prepare, eat, and clean up after breakfast and lunch. No student eats alone (Mckenzie 2017). The number of school days would be increased from 180 to 217 to match their parent's work schedule (see #Job Sharing and Increased Vacation Time).

Flip the Role of Classroom and Home

The present system has teachers making presentations to groups and then requiring them to write about it or practice at home. An alternative to this system is the "flipped" classroom where students watch videos or read texts at home and then use class time with teachers to practice. The prevalence of Internet connections and access to YouTube videos make it possible for students to watch presentations at home that are well designed and presented in an entertaining manner. Parents can insist that their children spend time watching or reading their assignments and can even watch the videos with their children. Parents would not be put in the position of trying to help their children with difficult concepts or topics with which they, the parents, are unfamiliar. It would also get parents out of the responsibility of doing their child's homework or projects for them. Students who have college-educated parents have a big advantage in the current system. It is much easier for parents with limited education to insist that a child spends a certain time watching required content, and it gives the parents a chance to learn along with their child.

When students do their writing or "homework" assignments is when they need the most expert help. Instead of spending their time sitting passively in a classroom watching the teacher, students would spend time in class practicing assignments or writing. When they need help, it would be available from the teacher who is a trained professional in that subject or a senior volunteer (see #Senior Service Corps). It would also assure that the student is doing the work and not their parents or their friends.

Make Schools Smaller

Larger schools have certain economies of scale and can offer more specialized subjects (and have more successful football teams), but there is a large cost in the development of children (Kokemuller, Neil 2016). Children can feel lost in big schools where most teachers or other students don't know their names. If we change our goal to helping students mature and to be happy in the process and if we

 Change the Role of Schools and Parents

adopt new teaching methods like the flipped classroom and longer school days, smaller schools become more practical.

I propose that we limit the size of schools to three hundred students. There are benefits and challenges to consider.

Transportation

Parents are fearful about letting their young children walk to school unsupervised even if they are less than a twenty-minute walk away. This deprives the student of exercise and an opportunity to converse with peers or siblings. US Service Corps people could be stationed at street corners before and after school in sufficient numbers to provide visual coverage of the entire route for many neighborhoods and older siblings could accompany young children (see #Koop on Prevention) (see #US Service Corps).

Parents need to be involved in schools, especially in early education. If an elementary school is located too far from home, it is more difficult for parents to serve during the day, and they often spend time driving children to school instead of letting them walk to school. If a school is too large, students and teachers lose a sense of community and teachers have difficulty controlling children they do not know.

I propose limiting school size to about three hundred students, including preschool through twelfth grade using Service Corps people to patrol streets while young children are walking to and from local schools or to man drop-off areas near schools where parents could drop children off safely but do it without too much waiting on the way to work.

Because the school day would be much longer than it is now, there would be time to transport students during the school day to aggregate groups in larger geographic areas for specialized classes or large group activity and to expose them to diverse experiences with students from other ethnicities and economic strata.

Home Economics and International Poor People's Food

Teenagers can learn to cook and maintain a home so that they can contribute to a household and become prepared to live on their own.

In this system, students would eat breakfast and lunch at school. This would be a good time to teach them how to read the ingredients list and how to construct a menu of foods that meet basic nutritional requirements. It would also be a good opportunity to teach them how to eat on a limited budget by introducing them to the kind of food that many people eat every day on other parts of the world that are low-cost, such as the following:

- Pasta and tomato sauce
- Tacos
- Beans and rice
- Stir-fry rice
- Asian noodles
- Soups and stews
- German spätzle and cheese
- Curry

New Teacher Qualifications

People who choose teaching as a profession do so with a clear idea of what it will be like based on what they observed when they were students. They want to work in education because they liked the experience and know how to succeed in that system to get a degree. The weakness of this arrangement is that teachers who go from the college classroom to their own K–12 classroom have not learned how to succeed outside of the education system, and they don't know what it is like in noncollege prep classes or how much teachers work at home. They are also attracted to the role of being the center of attention and having control of other people. Changing the education system will not succeed by imposing it from above on the existing faculty. The proposed system of longer school days will require teachers to be at school more hours, but that time can be used for preparation and homework grading, so they are done for the day when they head home.

I propose creating experimental schools that are designed from the ground up with the new goals mentioned above in mind.

This begins with choosing teachers who have the appropriate qualifications, experience, and personality. Teachers in the new schools would have

- five years of work experience outside of education;
- two years of public service such as the US Service Corps (see #US Service Corps);
- certification of subject matter expertise; and
- willingness to serve as a learning coach rather than be the center of attention.

Retrain or Replace Underperforming Teachers

When my oldest son was attending a large, highly rated high school in a university town, I was surprised to find out that geography was not a required part of his college preparatory program of study. I encouraged him to take a geography class, and he did as a sophomore. He was a bright and engaged student but started to complain about the quality of the class. He said the teacher was the track coach and hated football players like him. He also said that after six weeks, the class was still on the first chapter in the book. I went to parent-teacher night and met with the teacher. We were in a portable classroom building that is like a large mobile home. The first thing I noticed was that there were no maps on the walls in a geography class. When I asked him about this, he said that he had been reassigned from the main school building to one of these units, and the administration did not allocate any money to pay a custodian to hang the maps. As a protest, he refused to hang them himself or to teach the topics in the book. After I got over the impulse to strangle him, I realized that I was helpless as a parent to do anything about this other than get my son transferred.

I worked as a teacher at the high-school level for ten years and at the college level for thirty years and was a union member at both levels. I've walked more than one picket line, and the union won wage increases that made it practical for me to support my family as the primary bread winner, so I am not anti-union. However, in any large group, some of its members will have emotional or motivational problems that would get them fired in most business environments.

In the forty years I was a teacher, I did not know of one instance of a teacher being fired for poor job performance. The "punishment" available to administration for poor performance as a teacher was to assign them to noncollege prep classes where the parents were less likely to complain but where teaching expertise is even more important.

My eldest son is now a CEO, and he has had to fire several people. I asked him how he made that decision. He told me that if he could replace an employee with someone who could do the job better, it was his responsibility to make the change. It was that person's responsibility to find a job for which he or she was better suited or to make changes in their job skills. I'm not advocating that approach for teachers, but there needs to be a way to replace teachers who are not performing well with someone who is better and who is seeking work.

I propose giving parents a voice when a teacher is not doing a good job but which also protects academic freedom. For example, if the parents of 20 percent of the students file a petition calling for a review of a teacher's performance, the teacher would be placed on probation for a year. During that time, an experienced teacher would be assigned to mentor that teacher to help them improve or the teacher could take a semester leave at half pay to seek other employment. If the parents of 30 percent of the students sign a similar petition the following year, the teacher's tenure would be revoked and the administration could let the teacher go. Specific provision would be made in the rule to protect academic freedom so that objections to teaching topics like evolution or black history would not be considered grounds for dismissal.

US Service Corps in Schools

An immature child who is anxious or stressed does not make rational decisions. An anxious child under stress might act out and break the rules. The stress might come from an abusive home situation, bullying by peers, or many other sources that are unrelated to the rule that is broken, and punishment does not have a deterrent effect. If we recognize the school's role as helping the child to mature, we see that suspension is not the appropriate response to many acts of rule breaking.

I propose using volunteers from the US Service Corps who are only a few years older than the students to assist in providing a restorative-justice program in schools (see #US Service Corps):

> *Restorative justice (RJ) is a powerful approach to discipline that focuses on repairing harm through inclusive processes that engage all stakeholders. Implemented well, RJ shifts the focus of discipline from punishment to learning and from the individual to the community. (Ferlazzo 2016)*

US Service Corps members would receive basic training in RJ methods and assist school counselors and principals in helping students to make amends and restore a sense of community.

I also propose using US Service Corps people to improve school safety by monitoring school entrances, playgrounds, and hallways while wearing video cameras. Their role would be to report, record, provide witness, and call for help if necessary but not to intervene.

Emphasize Discernment and Thinking Skills

A few years ago, my wife asked me what I wanted for my birthday. I surprised her with an unusual request. I said that I wanted her to take my old slide rule from my college days and have it mounted so I could display it on my office wall. I graduated from the University of Michigan in 1968 with a major in physics (after transferring from engineering) and minors in mathematics and education. My class was the last to graduate before electronic calculators became available, so I did all my calculations with a slide rule. A slide rule can multiply, divide, and find square and cube roots and the value of trigonometric functions to three or four digits. However, it cannot tell you where the decimal point goes in the resulting number. This limitation forced me to develop methods of quickly estimating the size of the right answer to within a power of ten, so I knew where to put the decimal place in the answer. I've found this skill to be very valuable because it lets me catch large errors that people who grew up using calculators and computers often do not catch.

In today's information environment, it is often left up to the individual to identify when someone's argument is highly unlikely to be true—even if the numbers they quote are off by a factor of ten. Developing the skill that allows the individual to block exaggerations and lies before they become part of one's knowledge base takes training in logic as well as numerical estimating.

I propose that we teach basic logic and how to spot fallacies in everyday discourse. Here are a few examples (Williamson 2017):

> ***The A Priori Argument (****Also, Rationalization; Proof Texting.****):*** *A corrupt argument from logos, starting with a given, pre-set belief, dogma, doctrine, scripture verse, "fact" or conclusion and then searching for any reasonable or reasonable-sounding argument to rationalize, defend or justify it.*

> ***The Ad Hominem Argument*** *(also, "Personal attack," "Poisoning the well."): The fallacy of attempting to refute an argument by attacking the opposition's intelligence, morals, professional qualifications, personal character or reputation.*

> ***Alternative Truth:*** *A newly-famous contemporary fallacy of logos, denying the resilience of facts or truth as such. Writer Hannah Arendt, in her* <u>The Origins of Totalitarianism</u> *(1951) warned that "The ideal subject of totalitarian rule is not the convinced Nazi or the dedicated communist, but people for whom the distinction between fact and fiction, true and false, no longer exists."*

> ***The Big "But" Fallacy*** *(also, Special Pleading): The fallacy of enunciating a generally-accepted principle and then immediately negating it with a "but." Often this takes the form of the "Special Case," which is*

　　　　Emphasize Discernment and Thinking Skills

supposedly exempt from the usual rules of law, logic, morality, ethics or even credibility e.g., "As Americans we believe on principle that everyone has the inalienable right to a fair trial before a jury of his or her peers, but your crime was so unspeakable and a trial would be so problematic for national security that it justifies life in Guantanamo without trial or conviction."

The Big Lie Technique *(also the Bold-Faced Lie; "Staying on Message."): The contemporary fallacy of repeating a lie, fallacy, slogan, talking-point, nonsense-statement or deceptive half-truth over and over in different forms (particularly in the media) until it becomes part of daily discourse and people believe it without further proof or evidence.*

Teaching Science

In addition to logic, another major tool in the development of Western civilization is the scientific method of inquiry. Instead of arguing from authority, we learned to gather data, look for patterns, and then make and test hypothesis. The most important step in this process is the ability to conclude that a hypothesis is wrong and to try another hypothesis. Healthy skepticism—not cynicism—plays an important role in this process.

I observe some disturbing flaws in how many people teach science:

- Most text books focus on successes and not how the scientists dealt with failures.
- Laboratory experiments are intended to confirm known results.
- The role of healthy skepticism in developing hypotheses into theories is not taught.
- Images of famous scientists like Einstein do not portray them at the age when they made their discoveries.

The problem with teaching a series of scientific truths is that students don't learn how to recognize incorrect hypotheses and students learn to argue from authority instead of evaluating something for themselves. For example, you might hear the question: "Do you believe in evolution?" The word *believe* in this question indicates the person asking the question is accustomed to arguing from authority. The answer I would like to hear from a student would be, "One doesn't 'believe' in a scientific theory. I think the theory of evolution is the best explanation of the data we have. Here are some examples…"

The role of science education should be to give students the tools to think for themselves. If we simply argue that "scientists agree…" then it is an argument based on authority, and if someone accepts a religious source as their authority, they will not be persuaded. I think this explains why so many people in this country do not accept evolution or climate change in spite of the strongest possible support by science teachers.

I taught physics at the high-school level for ten years. When it came to lab experiments, I used to say, "You get a bachelor's degree in science to learn what the lab results should be. You get a master's degree to understand why the labs often don't give you those results." By this, I meant that there are complicating factors that hide the underlying principle you are trying to demonstrate and lab results in high school are often inconclusive. If the only way to get an A on a lab report is to get the expected data and confirm the principle behind the experiment, then our best and brightest students will produce those results—even if they have to scrub anomalous data from the lab report or even fake results.

One of my heroes of science is Johannes Kepler. He was a mathematician and astronomer in the age before the invention of the telescope. He had access to the meticulous observation of the motions of the planets in the night sky made by Tycho Brahe. Kepler assumed that heavenly objects would move through the heavens along circular paths whose spacing would be determined by nesting the circles within regular solids so the circles touched the corners or sides of regular solids. (A regular solid has faces that are the same shape and size like a cube.) Kepler devised a model of the solar system that combined spheres and regular solids such as cubes and three-sided pyramids that fit Brahe's data better than any other model (Hart 1998). The reason that he is one of my heroes is that he recognized that in spite of his best efforts, he couldn't get the model to fit the data to within the error limits of Tycho's observations, so he reexamined his assumptions and started over using ellipses (ovals) instead of circles, which turned out to be correct.

Another of the great stories of science is the Michelson-Morley experiment where they set out to prove the existence of an invisible fluid between the planets called the ether. Instead, they proved that it didn't exist! The scientific community awarded Michelson the Nobel Prize in Physics for the accuracy of his measurements on an experiment that didn't work.

When we confuse science with belief, we also confuse skepticism with heresy. In recent times, we've seen reports of "cold fusion" and particles that move faster than the speed of light (A. Cho 2012). Skeptical scientists examined the assumptions, procedures, and calculations of these reports and found enough irregularities to disqualify them as accepted fact. An important part of the scientific process is a requirement that someone who discovers something must persuade the skeptics with careful and rigorous work. The best way to convince a skeptic is to show that the results are repeatable and to use the hypothesis to predict something that is more than just an extrapolation of known trends. Fortunately, this type of success is easy for the nonspecialist to evaluate. We can teach students to ask two simple questions: "Can you do it again?" and "What unexpected or unknown data can it predict or discover?"

If we want to inspire teenagers to become scientists who discover new phenomena, cures, or theories, it is helpful if they can visualize it for themselves. When I taught physics, the only well-known physicist was Albert Einstein. Unfortunately, the image of him with which my students were familiar was a wild-haired, eccentric-looking old man (Albert Einstein's Quote n.d.). Instead, I put up a poster that showed what he looked like at their age and less of an authority figure (The Foundations of the New Physics 1900).

I propose changing the goal of science education from that of a factory designed to produce college students to a place where students learn to apply the scientific method of thinking, including healthy skepticism, so they can decide for themselves what to think and to use the scientific method to discover new relationships. The purpose is to reduce the practice of faking data to get an A, to shift from authoritarian arguments and *belief* in science to reasoning, and to judge the validity of new hypothesis for themselves.

Read and Write Future Fiction

New technologies can be used for good or ill, and it is important to consider the effects before they happen. Television had only been available for a few years in 1949 when George Orwell wrote *1984* in which he portrayed a world where the government leader known as *Big Brother* controlled everyone's lives. In his book, he envisioned televisions that had cameras in them to monitor everyone's behavior and the government could turn them on remotely and force everyone to start the day with exercise and pledges of obedience. Even the parks and woods were monitored with microphones, so there was nowhere anyone could be that was not under surveillance by the government. His view of a future only thirty-five years in the future was chilling. This book was required reading at many schools in the 50s and 60s, and when a government program sounded like it came from this future, the cry of *1984!* went up and people reconsidered. I recall a proposal by the city government of Ann Arbor, Michigan, to allow the government to turn on our televisions to warn us of weather threats like tornadoes. Many people said that it reminded them of Orwell's book, and they said they would rather take their chances with a tornado than give the local government the power to turn on our sets and make announcements of their choosing. Consider the relevance today of some of Orwell's statements from *1984*:

For, after all, how do we know that two and two make four? Or that the force of gravity works? Or that the past is unchangeable? If both the past and the external world exist only in the mind, and if the mind itself is controllable—what then?

Orthodoxy means not thinking—not needing to think. Orthodoxy is unconsciousness.

The Party seeks power entirely for its own sake. We are not interested in the good of others; we are interested solely in power, pure power.

To know and not to know, to be conscious of complete truthfulness while telling carefully constructed lies, to hold simultaneously two opinions which cancelled out, knowing them to be contradictory and believing in both of them, to use logic against logic, to repudiate morality while laying claim to it.

War is peace. Freedom is slavery. Ignorance is strength.

Big Brother is Watching You.

As you can see, this book's warnings about the future can be applied to today's world (Blakinger 2016), but this book is no longer required reading.

In addition to warning us about potential threats, we also must have time to decide how to apply our ethics and morals to new situations. We live in a world where technology is providing us with choices that we've never had before. One of the problems with this is that we have no experience to guide us, and our ethics and moral principles have not been applied to these issues before. It takes time to consider how to behave in these new circumstances, and we do not have enough time if we wait until they occur to think about it. For example, we might be on the verge of finding a cure for aging. What would be the effect on society? What would happen if the drug company charged $10 million for it?

I propose that we encourage students to read and write fiction about the future to sensitize them to risks and help them decide what would be the moral and ethical thing to do before they are faced with the choice.

Use Retirees to Teach Part Time

Grading homework can be converted into advising students on how to do better, but it takes more time to provide individualized feedback, especially in writing. This can be done by matching students up with retirees who are experienced teachers. About half of the teachers are expected to retire between 2009 and 2019, so it is likely that there would be many qualified people who would welcome the opportunity to become involved with a few individual students to read, respond, and evaluate their writing or other homework (Nation's Schools Facing Largest Teacher Retirement Wave in History 2011).

I propose that teachers work with the Senior Service Corps to coordinate retiree skills with teaching needs. Evaluations by these volunteers would be passed along to the managing teacher, the student, and the student's parents (see #Senior Service Corps).

Teacher Workload and Salaries

When I considered becoming a teacher in 1969 as the primary breadwinner, I had to consider the pay scale. My initial salary was low enough that I didn't have to move out of my federally subsidized housing, but the high end of the pay scale was as much as an engineer. An additional incentive was that I could get a draft deferment for teaching science. I switched majors from engineering to physics and picked up an additional minor in education to qualify for a teaching certificate. The pay scale went up each year based on years in service and additional education. I found the masters courses in physics to be particularly useful in teaching my classes. By the time I had two children, I could afford one car and a nice house with additional income from my wife who provided day care in our home, but still most of our children's clothes came from rummage sales. Along the way, we had two illegal strikes for higher pay in which I participated.

Today, the average teacher salary is about $57,000 plus about $19,000 (34 percent) for benefits or about $76,380 per teacher (Best Jobs: High School Teacher 2015; Luebke 2016). Teachers are required to work fewer days per year than most full-time employees—180 versus 245—and fewer hours per day—6.5 versus 8.5.

This sounds like a very nice job, but the attrition rate is high. About one in five washes out after one year and a third of new teachers don't last five years—about half in urban areas. Of the 269,800 teachers who left the profession in 2009, only 38 percent had made it to twenty years for full retirement (Nation's Schools Facing Largest Teacher Retirement Wave in History 2011).

I was one of those teachers who left high-school teaching after less than twenty years. I felt that I had the best job in the school district, but the acrimony between the union and the administration made the environment toxic. I reached the top of the pay scale and the limit of creative curriculum innovation—I increased enrollment in the physics courses by 460 percent. I wanted to try my wings in business, so I quit a tenured teaching job, cashed in my retirement equity, and started a computer-software business that specialized in energy audits. After three years, the business failed when the federal government required the utilities to give away the service we were selling. I combined my teaching and curriculum-development experience with additional education and my business experience to land a job as an assistant professor at a midlevel state university where I created degrees in energy and facility management and taught there for thirty years until my retirement in 2014. Teaching at the college level was much easier than teaching at the high-school level because I could focus on content rather than socialization and discipline.

When I was a professor, I had a discussion with another professor who taught polymer coating technology after working for twenty years in the industry. He had no experience teaching at the K–12 level, but he was critical of the quality of chemistry education taking place there. I explained to him that teaching the subject matter was the easy part of the job. I challenged him to work one day as a substitute teacher in the ninth grade in general education classes (not college prep). I bet him that he wouldn't make it to lunchtime. He didn't take the bet. The point of my bet is that teaching is often a very stressful job and that expertise in the subject matter is important, but it is not the key element in a teacher's success.

In my view, the average amount spent on teacher salaries and benefits is adequate, but distribution of that money needs to be changed, and the entire model of teaching must change to reduce stress and increase job satisfaction (see #Change the Role of Schools and Parents).

We promote equal pay for equal work when we advocate fair treatment of women versus men, but we do not support that value when we pay young teachers who are raising families less than older teachers for the same work.

I propose that we make the following changes to teacher workload and compensation:

- Remove the increase in pay for years of service.
- Keep the increase in pay for obtaining a master's degree in the teacher's major.
- Tie teacher pay to the number of student-hours for which they are responsible.
- Allow teachers to increase their income by managing teams of senior volunteers and US Service Corps volunteers to increase their productivity of student contact hours under their supervision (see #Senior Service Corps) (see #US Service Corps).
- Provide teachers with time during the extended school day to plan classes, report progress, and evaluate student progress (see #Change the Role of Schools and Parents). Teachers

should be done at the end of the day and not expected to work nights and weekends.

- Increase the number and length of school days from 180 to 217 to match the reduced full-time adult workload (see #Extend the School Day to Match Parent's Workday) (see #Job Sharing and Increased Vacation Time).
- Create a compensation board that compares teacher salary to those of other college graduates with similar degrees in the region and sets pay equal to the median of those salaries. Strikes would be illegal.

Teaching Reading, and Writing

Communicating by reading and writing is a critical skill, but teaching reading and writing can be the most time-intensive task a teacher can have. Experts still disagree about the best method to teach children to read. Most reading programs start with phonics where students relate the letters with sounds, but there are more than a billion Chinese who learn to read by memorizing the meaning of characters that provide no clue to their pronunciation (Phonics Basics 2017); (Upbin 2013). Clearly, our current methods do not work for everyone because thirty-two million (14 percent) of US adults cannot read, and the negative effect of illiteracy is indicated by the fact that 70 percent of prison inmates cannot read (Illiteracy Statistics 2016). For those students who are struggling with methods that work for the majority, one-on-one tutoring works if the tutor is a trained teacher (Effective Programs for Stuggling Readers: A Best Evidence Synthesis 2009).

The study cited above indicates that computer-assisted instruction programs were not effective for reading assistance, but all of us who have used a computer to write know how helpful the spell-check feature can be. Writing is a skill that is developed by doing it frequently and getting feedback on content and identifying and correcting spelling and grammar errors. Fortunately, modern word-processing software like Microsoft Word (MS Word) can identify most spelling errors with the notable exception of incorrect use of correctly spelled words such as *there, their*, and *they're*. A less well-known feature of MS Word is its grammar-checking feature (Look under File/Options/Proofing). This is an option that can be set to find and explain a long list of common grammatical errors, including the following (Select Grammar and Writing Style Options in Office 2016 2016):

- Adjective used instead of adverb
- Agreement with noun phrases
- Capitalization
- Comma splice
- Commonly confused words
- Comparative use
- Hyphenation
- Incorrect pronoun case
- Indefinite article
- Punctuation
- Spacing
- Subject-verb agreement
- Verb use
- Passive voice
- Double negation

Students could be required to use automatic spelling and grammar checking when they write and seek help as needed to understand the grammar rules. Emphasis should be shifted to writing skills that are harder to grade and correct automatically such as sentence structure. Volunteers could read and discuss the student's writing to provide feedback on structure, clarity of expression, and other more advanced writing skills.

I propose that we use retired teachers and other educated retirees to assist with reading and writing in our schools to provide the personal attention needed by those for whom the normal methods are not working and to increase the amount of writing all students are doing without increasing the workload of the teachers (see #Retirement) (see #Read and Write Future Fiction).

State-supported colleges typically charge lower tuition for residents of the state and much higher rates for out-of-state students. The difference is typically about $10,000 a year but might be much more (In-State vs. Out-of-State Tuition 2013). This creates a barrier for students who want to experience life in another part of the country. There are regional associations that allow students to attend public colleges in another nearby state for a discount, which lowers the barrier, but students are still restricted to schools that are in the same geographic region (Farah 2014).

I propose that we create an exchange process where students can attend any college in the country at the in-state tuition rate charged in their own state plus an adjustment factor to compensate states that provide more assistance to their public colleges. The exchange process would limit the number of students using the system to prevent a "brain drain" from a particular state. For example, if a student in Michigan wanted to attend a college in Alabama, he or she could do so for the in-state rate in Alabama if there is another student in Alabama who wants to go to school in Michigan and pay its in-state tuition.

The intent of this proposal is to reduce the regional misunderstandings within the country by exposing our future leaders to a broader range of cultural experiences.

Chapter Ten

Reorganize Prisons

There is something seriously wrong with our approach to dealing with criminal activity by incarcerating people. European countries have about one person per thousand in jail compared to seven per thousand in the United States (M. Y. Lee 2015). The average cost per prisoner in the United States is $31,286 a year, which means that if we cut our prison population down to levels found in Europe or the rest of the developed world, we would release almost two million people and save $60 billion a year (Santora, City's Annual Cost per Inmate is $168,000, Study Finds 2013).

It is important to be clear about the reasons for which we incarcerate people and design the institutions and their programs to address those reasons. These reasons include

- deterring crime and penalizing those who break laws;
- isolating people from society who pose a danger to the public;
- providing revenge for aggrieved parties in place of feuds, vendettas, and honor killings; and
- subjugating minorities and political dissidents.

Early Release through Slum Restoration

About five hundred thousand people are in jail for a nonviolent drug offense (Wagner and Rabuy 2016). Because a disproportionate percentage of those people are African American, some argue that the primary reason is to subjugate them as a minority. They point out that there are more black men in prison today than were enslaved in 1850 (Alexander 2010). Legalizing drugs, involving more young men in a service corps, and using restorative justice in schools rather than suspensions should dramatically reduce the inflow of new prisoners (see #Legalize Recreational and Addictive Drugs) (see #Create a Culture of Service and Higher Education).

In addition to reducing the inflow of new prisoners, we need a program that would release those who are serving sentences for acts that would no longer carry a jail sentence but that still recognizes that they broke the law and meet the objective of providing deterrence and punishment.

I propose that we create a one-year program to restore to the community those who are currently in prison for a nonviolent drug offense by creating a slum-restoration-work program. Aspects of the program are as follows:

- Local government would condemn buildings that are not being maintained and kept up to code and assume ownership if they are not repaired.
- Prisoners who qualify could volunteer for the program.
- Classes held in the prison would train them in basic house-renovation skills such as window replacement, scraping and painting, roofing, siding, and landscaping. Prisoners would have to demonstrate willingness to participate. The classes would last a month.
- Prisoners would work in supervised teams to clean up and repair condemned housing. They would wear GPS tracking units and return to prison in the evenings. If they escape, they would be charged with an additional crime and returned to the prison system.
- Local contractors would be paid to repair elevators, plumbing, and electrical systems and do structural repairs. Prisoners would have the opportunity to do some unskilled work alongside the contracted workers where they could become known to them as reliable workers.
- The prison supervisors and the contractors would evaluate the prisoners' effectiveness, attitude, and reliability. If they do not demonstrate or develop a good work ethic, they are returned to prison and may not reapply to the program for a year.
- Prisoners would be paid at a rate commensurate with an unskilled construction worker. The money would go into a dividend-paying stock fund (see #Payday Loans).
- At the end of the one-year program, if the prisoner has received acceptable evaluations, the prisoner is released. The

                    Early Release through Slum Restoration

former prisoner is given a certificate that attests to his or her ability to work effectively with others and he or she might be known to local contractors as a reliable worker. They would have access to enough money to meet an emergency from the dividends in the stock fund.

- The city could sell the housing to the prisoners who worked on them or its current tenants without a down payment for the amount they are currently paying as rent. Alternatively, the city could sell the housing and use the profits to fund the program (see Prison-Population Reduction and Slum Renewal).

Protection of Society

It would be nice to think that we know enough about psychology and drug therapy to expect that we can cure everyone, but that just isn't the case. It doesn't mean we should stop trying to do more for these people, but some of them are just too dangerous—especially to women and children—to be free. We also need to consider the harm they can do to each other and how stressful and damaging it is to prison guards who deal with them daily.

When I was a high-school teacher, one of our punishments was to require students to stay after school for an hour in a study hall that was supervised by a teacher. We took turns supervising this punishment period in pairs. It was supposed to be a study period, but few of these students brought books to read or homework to do. The main entertainment for them during this period was to see what they could get away with and how frustrated they could make the teacher. I learned from my more experienced colleague to make a deal with the students at the outset of the hour—if they behaved, we would let them out early. It was my introduction to the concept of using the possibility of parole to make life livable for prison guards. Without some reward for good behavior, these prisoners can make life very unpleasant for their jailers. Unfortunately, we also taught these students that the threat of misbehavior was effective in reducing their punishment.

For prisoners in this most dangerous category, I propose that we do not use parole as a trade-off for good behavior in prison because that might defeat the purpose of isolating them from the public. Instead, they would have a regular allotment of recreational drugs like marijuana that make the time pass more pleasantly and more passively. The supply of these drugs would be contingent on good behavior. I would not give up on rehabilitating these people, but the bar should be high to qualify for early release based on a diagnosis of recovery. Even with a diagnosis of recovery, these people would be monitored electronically, and the people who advocate their release would have to put up a bond and be personally responsible for their behavior.

Deterrence of Economic Crime

Some types of crime require rational forethought and are not a direct physical threat to the general public. People who consider the consequences of their actions might be deterred from acts such as embezzlement or theft. Some of those people will weigh the likely risk of getting caught against the reward or gratification of their acts and choose to take that risk. For these people, deterrence might work if the punishment was disagreeable enough or the risk outweighed the profit. In the past, inflicting pain by flogging and public shaming was used for this purpose.

Today, we make people pay fines or lock people in cages with other criminals for years. In some cases, the time they spend with other prisoners is an opportunity to learn from each other and to form relationships that continue after their release and result in coordinated criminal activity that is more efficient and harder to stop. On average, a criminal "earns" $11,000 a year more from illegal activity after prison (Vedantam 2013).

Another problem with incarcerating people for years is the cost to taxpayers. It costs taxpayers an average of $31,000 a year to house, feed, and guard a prisoner (Santora, City's Annual Cost per Inmate is $168,000, Study Finds 2013). Between the direct cost of prison ($31,000) and the indirect cost of increased theft ($11,000), the cost to the public is $42,000 a year. The punishment should be enough to deter a rational thief, and we should prevent criminals from using prison as a criminal university where they learn advanced methods of stealing.

Those convicted of stealing usually don't do long prison sentences, but being convicted of stealing goods worth more than $500 to $1,000 could result in a felony conviction that would make the person virtually unemployable. Without a job, many will steal again.

I propose that those who are convicted of stealing or embezzling take part in a restorative-justice program. Restorative justice has the following characteristics:

Restorative Justice reflects a belief that justice should, to the greatest degree possible, do five things (Sharpe 1998):

- Invite full participation and consensus
- Heal what has been broken
- Seek full and direct accountability
- Reunite what has been divided
- Strengthen the community, to prevent further harms

Some of the programs typically identified with restorative justice include the following:
- Victim/offender mediation or dialogue
- Conferencing
- Peace-making circles
- Victim assistance and involvement
- Former prisoner assistance and involvement
- Reduction of DMI (disparate minority incarceration)
- Real restitution
- Community service

The prisoners would take part in the slum-restoration program except that the money they earned would go toward making restitution for their crime. To be an effective deterrent, the amount they earn in the slum-restoration program would have to be greater than the amount they stole. If they do make full restoration by working, the felony would be reduced to a misdemeanor. While they are working on this program, they would be separated from other prisoners who stole property to reduce the opportunity to learn better techniques.

Revenge

Violent crimes often create a strong desire in the victims or their relatives for revenge. If those relatives kill or harm the person who harmed their loved one, a cycle of revenge killings can occur that are the source of feuds, vendettas, and honor killings that can go on for decades. To prevent that pattern from beginning, we treat violent crimes as offences against the state, and the government takes on the role of vengeance. This method gives some comfort to the relatives of the victim and removes that person from his or her locale where the relatives would be tempted to retaliate if they encountered the perpetrator.

Violent criminals are not only harmful to their first victims, but they can also harm other prisoners. They are also vulnerable to assault by prison staff (Wolff, et al. 2006).

I propose that incarceration of violent criminals be conducted with the following practices:

- Drugs are provided that have a calming effect like sedatives or marijuana for voluntary consumption that may be revoked for bad behavior.
- Victims or their blood relatives may testify at parole hearings and may veto early release. Restorative-justice programs would be available to prisoners who wish to appeal to the victims or their relatives for early release.
- Prison cells and common areas be monitored with video cameras equipped with infrared vision that can see in the dark.
- Prisoners are monitored on video by US Service workers to prevent sexual assault or other violence between prisoners and abuse by staff (see #US Service Corps).

Some people believe that private companies can do anything better than the government, which has led to the creation of companies that run prisons for a profit. Introducing a profit motive into the situation can result in the following problems:

- Profits might be increased by increasing crowding, lowering food quality, and paying less for staff salaries and benefits.
- Less experienced or poorly trained staff can lead to discipline problems between staff and inmates.
- Companies could spend some of their profits on political campaigns to support those who favor using their services or for sheriffs and judges who incarcerate more people for longer sentences (Margulies 2016).

If we are successful in dramatically reducing the prison population, we will have a surplus of facilities and prison employees.

I propose that operating and staffing the prisons be done by government employees in government-owned facilities, some of whom can be transitioned to managing slum-restoration-work crews.

Chapter Eleven

Change to Clean Energy

Qualitative thinking is needed when we are deciding what is the right thing to do. Quantitative thinking is needed when we are choosing between alternatives. To make the best decisions about energy, it takes both types of thinking. Here are some quantitative facts that must be considered:

- Consider a large football stadium like the "Big House" in Ann Arbor, Michigan, that holds about 110,000 people, and let's use that as a unit of measure. The US population is increasing by a "Big House" every month. About half the increase is due to immigration, and the other half is due to the difference between birth and death rates.

- World population is increasing by almost one "Big House" every day (Current World Population 2017).

- Populations of some developed countries like Japan and Europe have begun to decline giving hope that world population will peak when the rest of the countries become developed. In the short term, world population is expected to increase by more than two billion people in the next thirty years (World Population Projected to Reach 9.7 Billion by 2050 2015).

- These projections do not include the effect of discoveries that would eliminate disease or extend life like the gene drive that might stop malaria or new cures for cancer or aging (Saplakoglu 2017).

- To reduce pollution from burning fossil fuels by conservation or replacement with solar or wind, the contribution from these methods and sources must be greater than the increase in population to make any reduction at all.

- Wind and solar are highly variable and need storage devices to offset the variability.

When we try to project our growth rate into the future, there are two broadly different ways to think about it. The first is to assume the earth is an open system into which an abundant new source of energy (fossil fuels) has been introduced that will continue indefinitely. The second is to assume the earth is a closed system with finite amounts of resources and limits to the amount of waste that can be absorbed or recycled.

Projections of world population of eleven billion and above are based on the first assumption. Even though we know that the fossil fuels that took millions of years to accumulate will be used up in a few centuries, we assume we will find new deposits for at least our lifetimes and those of our children, which is probably the case, and when they do start to run out, it will be a gradual decline that will give us time to change to other sources when necessary.

The second type of system is of more immediate concern. We know that biological organisms in a closed system that are exposed to an abundance of new resources will increase in population exponentially (as we have done) until one of the necessary resources is exhausted or the population's waste products poison its food and water supply at which point the population crashes in a sudden die-off.

Resource Depletion

The two resources of which I'm aware that might run out completely and unexpectedly are underground water and ocean fish.

Aquifer Depletion

We pump water from underground basins called aquifers to irrigate our crops. If we take out more than what accumulates from rainfall, the level of water goes down, but since it is underground, the drop in level can go unnoticed. For example, the Ogallala aquifer is an underground body of water that lies under eight states from South Dakota to Texas. If it were above ground, it would be bigger than the Great Lakes combined. Water is pumped out of the aquifer to grow about one-fifth of US cattle, corn, cotton, and wheat. The aquifer is already down by 30 percent and is expected to be down another 39 percent in fifty years (Bjerga 2015). Imagine the public outcry if the Great Lakes were being depleted at a similar rate. New satellite data show that half of the world's aquifers are declining while supporting the present population of seven billion people (Frankel 2015). Adding billions to the earth's population will certainly accelerate this depletion.

Ocean-Fish Depletion

The other out-of-sight resource that could decline unexpectedly is the ocean fisheries. The decline in food output from the oceans has been offset by improved methods of finding fish and being able to find them in remote parts of the ocean. When those areas are depleted, the output could drop suddenly. Fish farming depends on catching smaller fish in the wild and feeding them to the larger fish in captivity. Large fish eat twenty times their weight in smaller fish, so fish farming leads to depletion of fish further down the food chain until they run out (Vince 2012).

If the world population does peak at around eleven billion and then declines to more sustainable levels, we need a way to get through that period without running out of food or poisoning ourselves in our own waste products. The good news is that there are clean alternatives to fossil fuels that have enough energy to desalinate ocean water so that deserts may be farmed and wastewater purified.

Here are some ideas for generating large amounts of clean energy.

Wind, Solar, and Electric Cars

Automobiles pose a special challenge to clean energy because the energy source must be small and lightweight enough to fit in a car. We use liquid fuels and internal combustion engines to power our cars and trucks, but it is much harder to control the pollution from exploding gasses in an engine than it is from a steady flame in a power plant. We can reduce the emissions from burning fossil fuels for automobile transportation by generating electricity in a highly controlled environment and storing the energy in batteries in the cars. We can eliminate the pollution entirely if we can generate electricity without burning fossil fuels.

Solar energy is only available on earth for half a day and then sporadically during daytime due to cloud cover. For example, the seventy-two thousand solar panels at Nellis Air Force Base in the California desert have a capacity factor (actual energy produced/full energy output 24/7) of about 24 percent. In areas with more cloud cover like southeast Michigan, the capacity factor of solar panels is even less at about 10 percent.

Wind turbines can produce power any time the wind blows, but their energy output is even more variable than solar panels because the power output of a wind turbine varies with the cube of the wind speed (Kalmikov and Dykes n.d.). This means that if a wind turbine is rated at 1,000 kilowatts of power output at a wind speed of 20 mph, it will only produce one-eighth of that (250 kilowatts) at a wind speed of 10 mph ($1/2 \times 1/2 \times 1/2$). The result is a highly variable source that needs buffering if it is to be connected to the grid in large quantities.

To make use of solar and wind to replace fossil fuels, they need to be paired with storage devices that absorb their variability. This is hard to do on a large scale. A few utilities like those in Michigan and North Carolina pump water uphill into reservoirs when they have extra power and let it generate electricity by flowing downhill through generators when they need it, but geography limits that option (Ludington Pumped Storage 2017); (Pumped-Storage Hydro Plants n.d.).

The good news is that there have been big advances in battery technology. It is possible to store enough energy in a car battery to give it a range of 265 miles (Straubel 2014). I own a Chevy Volt, which is powered by a battery that has a range of about 36 miles on a full charge and a small gasoline engine that has a range of 380 miles on ten gallons of gasoline. Because most of my trips are less than 36 miles, I might go for months without stopping at a gas station because I recharge the battery from my household electricity each night.

Car manufacturers like Chevrolet and Tesla offer warrantees on their car's batteries, and they want to control how they are used very carefully to avoid shortening their life. Consequently, you can only charge the car battery from the household electricity. If you have a power failure, you cannot use the battery in your car to power your house until utility power is restored. When I lose power from the utility at my home, I run a gasoline-powered generator even though I have a fully charged battery in my car that could run the house for half a day or indefinitely with the engine running.

There is a similar problem with solar and wind installations that are connected to the utility power lines. I am a member of the First Unitarian Congregation of Ann Arbor, and this group spent more than $100,000 to install fifteen kilowatts of solar- and wind-generating equipment. In the fall of 2016, a transformer blew out on the utility's lines. The church had no power at all, not even enough to run the water pumps needed to provide water to the restrooms, so the church had to close on a Sunday morning. I found out that the contract with DTE Energy specified that all the energy produced be fed into the utility's power lines. We had no battery storage or means to disconnect from the utility and power the building's systems independently. This arrangement allows the utility to fulfill a state mandate that the utility have 15 percent of its generating capacity provided by solar or wind (Pyper 2016).

The two problems mentioned previously are not technical. They could be resolved by setting government standards for interconnecting utility power with alternatives and storage batteries.

I propose setting standards for equipment that would facilitate interconnection between storage batteries in cars and solar-and wind-generation systems at home and at work and then replacing flat roofs on commercial buildings with solar roofing materials and connecting them to changing ports in the parking lot and to the utility grid.

Imagine a future where you would have two batteries. One would hang on the wall in the garage, and another would be in the car. The battery in the garage would charge up from solar roofing materials that look like normal shingles and be available to charge your car at night or run your home (Solar Roof 2017). You could charge up your car at night in the garage from surplus utility capacity, wind power, or stored solar power from your house battery. You could drive to work on a summer's day in a silent vehicle that does not create smog, and when you arrive, you could plug in at a parking space where your car would be connected to the company's solar panels on the big flat roof of their building. You could top off your car's battery in the morning from the company's solar panels, and then in the afternoon when the building's air-conditioning system is demanding the greatest amount of electricity of the day, you could give or sell some of it back to the company and keep enough to run errands and get home.

For example, motorists in Michigan drive about ninety-seven million miles a year. An electric car gets about four miles per kilowatt-hour, so it would take about twenty-four million Kwh of electricity to replace the gasoline and diesel fuel used in Michigan. A solar panel in cloudy Michigan can produce 0.05 Kwh per day per square foot, so it would take about 480,000,000 square feet or about 17 square miles of solar panels. If we use solar panels, they could be solar roofing material on flat building roofs in an area only 4 miles square (square root of 17 = 4.1). Next time you fly over an urban area, look at all the flat roof buildings.

We have all the technology. We just need coordination and connection standards from the government. We could do this now!

BusTrains for Mass Transit

Another way to reduce the use of fossil fuel and clean up the air in cities is to use the highways more efficiently and reduce the number of automobiles by half.

I had a nice discussion with a person who works at the National Transportation Safety Board—the group that investigates transportation accidents—during which I asked what he thought about driverless cars. He said that he thought the technology would work its way into the mainstream in stages, beginning with accident avoidance systems (About the National Transportation Safety Board 2017).

We already have systems that can detect lane changes and brake automatically to avoid rear-end collisions and pedestrians. We may soon see systems that communicate between cars to avoid T-bone collisions at intersections and allow cars to drive closer together at full speed on freeways. As people become accustomed to automated features in cars that take over command decisions to avoid accidents, and if they perform well to earn our trust, the "driverless car" will become a reality.

We have an opportunity to combine the new, automated driving-control systems with existing infrastructure to revolutionize mass transit systems.

For mass transit to become a popular alternative to driving one's own car, it must have the following features:

- Costs less
- Gets you to your destination faster or at least as fast
- Makes better use of your time during transit

Many people look to Europe as a model of mass transit with its network of trains, subways, and buses. This model works well if there is a high density of population, and the right-of-way for trains was created while the cities grew. It is very difficult and expensive to create new transportation corridors in existing cities like those in the United States that grew up using automobiles instead of trains. To make a mass transit system that costs less than using personal vehicles, we must use the existing freeway infrastructure as much as possible. There is a light-duty vehicle for every driver in the United States and an average of two vehicles per household (Cohn 2013). The big savings would be made if we could cut that number in half by making it easier to get where we want to go with only one vehicle per family.

One of the things to recognize about the speed of mass transit is that the limiting factor is not the top speed of the conveyance but the number of stops it makes. To get from your home to work faster or at least as fast as driving your own car, you need to use a system that minimizes the number of stops, especially during rush hour.

One day I was driving on the freeway in Chicago during rush hour, and an advertisement on the radio caught my attention. It began with a man talking to himself while driving home from work. As he got stuck in traffic or was cut off by another driver, he became increasingly angry and frustrated until he was shouting. The ad ended with the question: "This is your husband on the way home from work. Wouldn't it be nicer if he took the train?" The same question could be asked of this man's employer about his worker's state of mind upon arriving at work. Driving your own car during rush hour is a form of work. Commuting to work adds an additional four hours to the average American's workweek (Stringer 2015). An effective mass transit system could make those hours productive or at least less stressful.

I propose that we create a transportation system that uses our freeways with a special BusTrain© in combination with local transfer buses and on-call car services or driverless cars. Consider the following scenario:

Home to Local Bus Transfer Station

Instead of having two cars, the family has one car where one of the drivers in the family spends the day at a distant work location to which he or she must commute, while the other person works at home, more locally, or commutes on a different schedule. The commuter drives the family car to the bus-transfer station. A smartphone app informs the driver when the next bus will arrive, to minimize waiting. He or she instructs the driverless car to return home before the other driver needs it or when local traffic is light. The car waits until traffic is light and makes its way home where it is available all day to the other driver in the household.

Local Bus Transfer to a BusTrain

At the bus-transfer station, the commuter boards a transfer bus that drives to the nearest freeway where it mates with a BusTrain. The transfer bus and the BusTrain are equipped with docking ports, and when the transfer bus pulls up behind the BusTrain, automatic speed controls take over and bring the two vehicles together like jet airplanes refueling in midair. The doors open, and passengers transfer between them. The transfer bus disconnects and then drops passengers off at the next transfer station.

BusTrain

A BusTrain is designed to travel at the highest practical speed on the freeway using HOV lanes where available. Because it has automated sensors and collision-avoidance systems, it can even drive on the paved shoulder at higher speed than would normally be safe to bypass traffic jams and maintain speed. It does not make local stops. While on the BusTrain, the commuter would relax or begin the day's work by connecting his or her laptop to the Internet via an onboard wireless network.

Transfer from BusTrain to Downtown Transfer Bus

When the BusTrain gets close to the commuter's destination and the next transfer bus is docked, he or she walks from the BusTrain into the transfer bus.

On-Call Vehicle to Work

While the transfer bus is making its way from the freeway to the transfer station, the commuter uses his or her smartphone to contact an on-call service such as Uber or Lyft to arrange a ride. When the transfer bus arrives at the transfer bus station, a car is waiting to take him or her directly to work without having to find or pay for parking or having to walk from the parking lot to the place of work.

The commute from work to home would be the reverse scenario, except the car owned by the family could drive itself to the transfer station to pick up the commuter.

The cost to own and operate a vehicle that you drive fifteen thousand miles a year is about $8,800 (Annual Cost to Own and

Operate a Vehicle Falls to $8,798, Finds AAA 2015). If a family can do with one less car by using mass transit, that would free up $167 per week. If the cost of the bus ride is $15 plus a $6 Uber ride, it would cost $105 for a five-day workweek for a savings of $62 a week or $248 a month, not counting parking fees. (The break-even cost would be $33 a day for bus plus Uber fees.)

In summary, this BusTrain plus on-call vehicle system would cost less, get you to work faster, and allow you to work or relax during the ride.

Thorium Nuclear Energy

"The stone age did not end for lack of stone" (Frei 2008). This is a famous quotation from the Saudi oil minister, Sheik Yamani, who foresaw a day when technology would make oil obsolete. We were at the brink of that era in the 1940s but took a wrong turn. The story of that choice is not well known. It is like a combination of *Jurassic Park* and *Raiders of the Lost Ark*. Like *Jurassic Park*, scientists were trying to bring back something from Earth's prehistoric past and inadvertently unleashed a force that could destroy humanity. Like *Raiders of the Lost Ark*, it involved Nazis, covert ops, and a fight for world domination. The difference is that it really happened. It goes like this:

When stars explode, they crush atoms together to make larger than normal atoms. These large atoms are unstable and spit out small parts of themselves several times until they get small enough to become stable. Some of them do this in a matter of a few years while others take billions of years. The rate at which they spit out parts is called the *half-life*, which indicates how long it takes for half of the atoms to do this. (In the next half-life, half of what is left will do it and so on until too little is left to find.)

We think that it has been about 4 billion years since our sun and its planets were formed from an aggregation of the remains of previously exploded stars. The largest type of atom that is still found on earth is uranium. It has a half-life of 4.5 billion years, so a little more than half of the original amount is still here. The third largest atom is thorium, which has a half-life of 14 billion years, so more of the original thorium is still here.

Scientists discovered that atoms could be fundamentally changed by bombarding them with uncharged particles called *neutrons*. The unusual result of bombarding an atom with neutrons is that if the neutron sticks, it can transform the atom into a different, larger atom.

In the 1930s, the best atomic scientists in the world were in Germany, which had been taken over by the Nazi party. A German scientist named Otto decided to see if he could recreate atoms that might have existed in the prehistoric past but which had shorter half-lives than uranium or thorium and had since disappeared. He set about bombarding uranium with neutrons to try and recreate these atoms that had vanished before dinosaurs had walked the earth and that had completely unknown properties. What could go wrong!

This procedure had two results, including the one that was intended. He did succeed in creating an element that had vanished from the earth, and it is named plutonium. The unintended result that Otto didn't understand was that some of the uranium atoms split apart into much smaller atoms in one step and spit out several neutrons at the same time.

Because the Nazis controlled Germany at the time, they threatened to imprison or kill any Jews they could find, including Otto's research partner, Lisa. Otto wasn't a bad guy. He gave Lisa some of his family jewelry with which to bribe the border guards, and she fled to Sweden. Otto and Lisa pondered the results of their experiments by phone, and they finally recognized the unintended result, which they called *fission* (Tretkoff 2017). The big deal about the fission of Uranium in a single step is that a lot of energy is released all at once, and it also emits neutrons that can cause other uranium atoms to fission in a *chain reaction*. The amount of energy released is mind-boggling. It is a hundred million times greater per atom than the most violent chemical reactions like dynamite or TNT. They had discovered an explosive power that was great enough to destroy an entire city with one bomb.

The idea that Nazi Germany had discovered a material that could be made into a super-weapon deeply frightened the US government. The good news was that it wasn't easy to do and would take a big effort to move this discovery from the laboratory to the battlefield.

Uranium comes in different "types" called *isotopes*. The difference in isotopes is the number of neutrons already in the atom. Uranium has 92 positively charged parts called *protons*, but an atom of uranium can have a range of neutrons, which also determines the half-life and ability to fission. The sum of the number of protons and neutrons in the atom is its *mass number*. For example, all uranium atoms have 92 protons. The most common isotope of uranium has 146 neutrons and its mass number is 238 (92 + 146). The isotope of uranium that can fission has 143 neutrons with a mass number of 235. Uranium 235 has a half-life of less than one billion years (seven hundred million), so much less of it is left from when the earth was formed—less than 1 percent of the uranium is U-235.

Because more than 99 percent of the uranium is U-238 and it doesn't fission, it gets in the way of the interaction between the atoms of U-235. To get enough U-235 concentrated into a small enough space so that the neutrons spit out during fission can cause other U-235 atoms to fission, the percentage must be increased or *enriched*. This is hard to do because the isotopes of uranium are chemically identical, so the only way to change the ratio is to use the small difference in mass between 235 and 238. One way to do this is to make the uranium into a gas by combining it with fluorine gas and then spinning it in a centrifuge. To get enough to make a bomb, it takes months of spinning in thousands of centrifuges, and you only get enough for one bomb.

Remember plutonium? It was made by bombarding the more plentiful uranium-238 with neutrons. One of its isotopes, Pu-239, will also fission like U-235 and can be made into bombs. A factory-scale effort was launched in America to produce enough enriched uranium to make a chain reaction that produced lots of neutrons. The neutrons could be used to transform U-238 into Pu-239.

Because plutonium is a different element, it can be separated and concentrated using chemistry instead of centrifuges. This project was called the Manhattan Project. The purpose of this project was to produce nuclear weapons before the Nazis could do it. It was successful in meeting that goal. The Nazis lost the war before the bombs were ready, but the bombs were used to end the war with Japan.

The first bomb we used was made with enriched uranium, and the others made since then use plutonium-239 that include traces of plutonium-240, both of which are created by transforming U-238. The small amount of Pu-240 causes problems because it will fission spontaneously, so bombs made with plutonium need a more sophisticated design with hollow spheres of plutonium that are crushed by shaped explosive charges. Making these shaped charges implode perfectly is also difficult, but several countries have mastered the technique. The world now has tens of thousands of nuclear bombs made with plutonium. Makes an island full of dinosaurs look pretty tame, doesn't it?

While this race to create a doomsday weapon was going on, there was another line of research at the Manhattan Project that used neutrons from a uranium-235 reaction to transform the more plentiful thorium into uranium-233 that can also fission. They discovered that U-233 didn't make good bombs and the process didn't produce plutonium, so the thorium/uranium process was not pursued.

After World War II, the government wanted to find a peaceful use of atomic energy. Remember the wrong turn I mentioned before? This is where it happened. Because the Manhattan Project had developed a lot of knowledge and expertise in the manufacture and use of uranium-235 and plutonium-239 for weapons, they reasoned that they should use that knowledge for generating electricity, which they did. While the uranium/plutonium process is great for making a lot of bombs, it has some significant drawbacks for making electricity. Here are a few:

- Uranium-235 is as scarce as platinum.
- Reactors that use heat from the fission of U-235 also transform some U-238 into Pu-239 and Pu-240.
- The Pu-239 can be extracted from used fuel rods and made into bombs.
- The Pu-240 has a half-life of sixty-five hundred years and continues to spontaneously fission in used fuel rods producing heat that needs continuous cooling.
- U-235 reactors use water to slow the neutrons so they cause fission more frequently and to make high-pressure steam that produces electricity. The use of high-pressure steam requires large, strong containment buildings to contain a breech.
- Loss of continuous external cooling can cause meltdowns of the solid fuel into gasses that can escape the containment building or explode.

There was another choice available—the thorium/U-233 process uses a completely different design. Instead of solid fuel pellets, thorium is combined with fluorine to make a salt that is solid like rock salt at room temperature. The thorium salt is heated and melted and exposed to the neutrons in a U-235 reactor to get it started. Some of the thorium is transformed into uranium-233. Once the U-233 starts to fission, it produces its own neutrons that can continue the chain reaction and transform more of the thorium into U-233. This type of reactor is known by the acronym LFTR, pronounced *lifter*, that stands for *Liquid Fluorine Thorium Reactor*. Here are some advantages of the LFTR reactor (Sorensen 2014):

- Thorium is a common element.
- A LFTR doesn't produce plutonium-239 that can be made into bombs.

- A LFTR doesn't produce Pu-240, so its used fuel is safer to store and loses its activity in a few human lifetimes instead of thousands of years.
- Molten salt doesn't require a large, strong containment building like high-pressure steam.
- The speed of the neutrons from fission of U-233 is in the right range for making U-233 fission and for transforming thorium into U-233.
- It is already melted, so it doesn't "melt down." Instead, if operating power is lost, the liquid fuel will drain by gravity into a holding tank where the fission stops and the salt hardens into a solid that is easily contained.

I propose that we retrace our steps and go back to that decision we made in 1945 and launch a major research effort to develop atomic power based on thorium. Here are some reasons to do this:

- Atomic fission produces a hundred-million times more energy per atom than the most violent chemical explosion or from fossil fuels and a billion times more energy per atom than wind.
- The amount of thorium fuel needed to provide a person with all the energy he or she needs for an entire lifetime would fit in the palm of your hand—and so would its waste.
- The small amount of waste would need to be isolated from people for two or three human lifetimes, not thousands of years because it doesn't contain Pu-240.
- LFTRs can be smaller. A reactor that would power a city could fit in a small building like the power plants at airports or college campuses, and the waste heat could be used to heat nearby buildings instead of dumped into the air or lakes.
- We are the best in the world at high-tech manufacturing. We could build LFTRs for export that would provide high-paid jobs for American workers and increase our influence in the developing world.
- It isn't easy or proven technology. But that means that whoever figures out how to do it first will own the patents.

That is why China has seven hundred nuclear engineers working on a molten-salt reactor (Martin, China Details Next-gen Nuclear Reactor Program 2015).

There are an additional two billion people coming in the next thirty years with two billion more on the way after that. LFTRs could be used to provide clean energy to desalinate ocean water, make deserts bloom, feed the next four billion people, and save the world from running out of fresh water and food or from poisoning itself on waste products. We have enough time to meet that challenge and take advantage of it if we have the right leadership and the will to do it.

The United States spends almost $500 billion on science and technology research and development, but a majority of that is from business, which is generally focused on the short-term development of products rather than long-range basic research that leads to fundamental advances (US R&D Spending at an All-time High, Federal Share Reaches Record Low 2016).

China is increasing its investment in science and technology at an annual rate of 19.5 percent and is expected to exceed R&D spending by the United States by 2022 (Report: U.S. global lead in R&D at risk as China rises 2016). China is investing heavily in energy technologies of all types, including nuclear. The United States has ninety-nine nuclear reactors producing about four gigawatts of electric power, with only two new reactors under construction (Plumer 2017). China has thirty-four reactors and plans to build thirty new reactors of traditional design while developing inherently safer new designs. One of these is the molten-salt reactor design that can consume used fuel rods from existing reactors or thorium (Martin, Fail-Safe Nuclear Power 2016).

Chapter Twelve

Whenever I'm watching a football game in which one of the teams has a large lead and the coach decides to abandon the game plan that got the team to that point and go into a "prevent defense" I shout at the TV and yell, "Don't do it. You'll lose your momentum!"

Perhaps you've heard of Hadrian's wall. It is a wall that the Romans built across Scotland, and it was the high-water mark of the Roman Empire (Breeze n.d.). The most famous wall is the Great Wall of China, which was constructed to keep out the barbaric tribes from the north. The Mongols broke through the wall in 1214 and took over China (Cavendish 2015). More recently, the French built a wall in the 1930s—the Maginot line—to keep out the Germans. The Germans simply drove around the end of the wall and defeated the French in a few weeks (Maginot Line 2009). To me, building a wall is a sign of fear and a loss of confidence in the "game plan" that made your country great. It's the equivalent of using a "prevent defense."

The population of the world is growing by about 110,000 people per day. That's one large college football stadium full of people. The US population is growing by about 110,000 people per month or one large stadium worth (Growth Rate 2017). The growth of US population is due to two factors: the death rate is lower than the birth rate (one new birth per eight seconds and one death every eleven seconds) and a net migration of one immigrant per sixteen seconds (U.S. and World Population Clock 2017).

As women become better educated and have access to birth control and fewer children die young, women choose to have fewer children (Nargund 2009). We see this occurring in Western Europe, Japan, and the United States. As the population elsewhere increases faster than the United States, the difference becomes greater and the issue of immigration and citizenship more important. It is like a difference in water level; as the difference increases, so does the pressure difference. Rather than build a seawall that must be continually heightened, I suggest that we take steps to decrease that pressure difference that are both short-term and long-term. People don't want to uproot their families and move to another country unless they are desperate or are ambitious. We benefit by accepting the ambitious. We should look to solve this problem by addressing the problems that make people desperate.

Support International Family Planning

An effective way to reduce population growth is to provide women with education and means to control their own fertility. President Eisenhower said this:

> *"Governments must act and private citizens cooperate urgently through voluntary means to secure this right for all people," he said. "Failure would limit the expectation of future generations to abject poverty and suffering and bring down upon us history's condemnation." (Birth Control 'for All People' 1993)*

Consider the table below. It shows that prior to President Reagan, the Republicans were the party that favored birth-control education as part of our foreign policy. President Reagan linked abortion with federal aid for family planning in the Mexico City Policy of 1984, and it has been a partisan issue since then.

President	*Position on Aid for Birth Control in Foreign Countries*
Eisenhower '53–'61	In favor (*New York Times* 1993)
Kennedy '61–'63	Not in favor but would go along with Congress (Time 1959)
Johnson '63–'69	In favor (Lyndon B. Johnson 1968)
Nixon '69–'74	In favor (The Center for Research on Population and Security 1993)
Ford '74–'77	In favor (The Center for Research on Population and Security 1993)

Carter '77–'81	Withdrew support (The Center for Research on Population and Security 1993)
Reagan '81–'89	Strongly against. Mexico City Policy (*New York Times* 1993)
Bush, George H. W. '89–'93	Against (*New York Times* 1993)
Clinton '93–'01	In favor
Bush, George W. '01–'08	Against
Obama '09–'16	In favor
Trump '17–	Against

I propose that we separate the issue of abortion from the other issues of family planning and provide information and pregnancy prevention assistance to avoid, in the words of President Eisenhower, "history's condemnation."

Improve Lives in Other Countries

Another factor that fuels immigration is the disparity between income. Fortunately, we have enjoyed a period of relative peace and prosperity since World War II. In the United States, our discussions have been focused on the effects of world trade as they affect our workers. The negative effect is real, but we should recognize that the positive effect on the poorest people in the world has been dramatically positive. World poverty is declining and might be eliminated. Bill Gates predicts that world poverty will be eliminated by 2035 and that a significant part of that progress is due to foreign aid:

> *I am optimistic enough about this that I am willing*
> *to make a prediction. By 2035, there will be almost*
> *no poor countries left in the world. (I mean by our*
> *current definition of poor.) Almost all countries*

> *will be what we now call lower-middle income or richer. (Gates 2017)*

I propose that we continue to engage in world trade to improve the lives of the world's poorest people who also have the highest birth rates but protect American workers.

Manage Exit Visas

About 40 percent of illegal immigrants do not climb or tunnel under a wall—they arrive legally for a temporary visit and then don't leave. We check incoming visitors at air- and seaports and at vehicle-entry points to be sure that they have proper paperwork, but we don't check to be sure that they leave. This problem was recognized as early as 1981 by the Select Commission on Immigration and Refugee Policy and restated by the 9/11 Commission when the commission recommended that the Department of Homeland Security:

> *... should complete, as quickly as possible, a biometric entry-exit screening system, including a single system for speeding qualified travelers. (Entry-Exit System: Progress, Challenges, and Outlook 2014)*

This seems to me to be low-hanging fruit. Before we spend a lot of money trying to keep people out, let's spend money tracking the people who are here legally but temporarily and make sure they leave when they are supposed to.

I propose that we follow the recommendations of the two earlier commissions and institute exit controls to greatly reduce the 40 percent of illegal immigration that begins as legal entry.

Citizenship

While we are waiting for population pressure to equalize due to slowing population growth and diminished difference in income, we need to make some adjustments to our citizenship and immigration laws.

Citizenship by Birth

The simplest way to become a citizen of the United States is to be born here. Our present policy grants citizen status to a newborn child even if neither parent is a citizen and they crossed the border without permission (US Citizenship 2013). We even grant citizenship to tourists who give birth while in this country (Kim and Shyong 2017). This policy provides a powerful incentive for noncitizens to enter the United States before a child is born. I think we need to remove that incentive.

I propose that we stop granting citizenship based solely on birthplace within the United States and only grant citizenship to children who have at least one parent who is a US citizen and who can provide DNA proof of parenthood. One of the parents who is a citizen must acknowledge financial responsibility for the child until the age of eighteen. The intent of this proposal is to eliminate sperm donors and surrogate mothers from conferring citizenship.

Citizenship for Parents of Citizens

We need a method to allow those who came here without permission and who have given birth to children who are now citizens under existing law a way to become citizens and also make amends for breaking the law.

I propose that a person who has a child who is a US citizen by birth be allowed to gain citizenship by serving for two years in the military or one of the service corps (see <u>#Create a Culture of Service and Higher Education</u>). A family member, such as a child who has citizenship by birth, may serve the two years in that person's place.

Citizenship for Illegal Residents

Those who overstayed their visas or who crossed the border illegally within the last five years must return to their country of origin or apply for asylum. Those who have been in the country for more than five years and who have a letter from an employer stating that they are providing a necessary service may apply for citizenship. Because they violated the law, they must work in one of the services for four years. If they are unwilling to do so, they must return to their country of origin or apply for asylum.

Legal Immigrants Serve Two Years

Those who are born in other countries and who have qualified for entry to this country according to our laws would be better integrated into our culture if they spent time meeting people from around the country and visiting many different parts of it.

I propose that immigrants be required to serve two years in the US Service Corps to finalize their status as citizens (see #US Service Corps).

Wall with Mexico

According to the US Census and the 2014 Mexican National Survey of Demographic Dynamics (ENADID), between 1965 and 2015, more than 16 million Mexicans immigrated to the United States. The flow of migrants peaked in 2007 and then reversed following the economic problems of 2008. Between 2009 and 2014, 1 million Mexicans and their families left the United States for Mexico, while 870,000 Mexicans immigrated to the United States. The Mexican-born population in the United States peaked in 2007 at 12.8 million and fell to 11.7 million by 2014 (Gonzales-Barrera 2015).

One of the issues in the 2016 presidential campaign was the need to build a wall across the border between the United States and Mexico. To build a forty-foot high wall would cost about $15 billion not including labor and land, which would bring the total to about $25 billion, which is $77 per US citizen (Farber 2017).

During his candidacy, Donald Trump proposed building a wall and that he would make Mexico pay for it:

> *I will build a great wall—and nobody builds walls better than me, believe me—and I'll build them very inexpensively. I will build a great, great wall on our southern border, and I will make Mexico pay for that wall. Mark my words. (Trump, I'll Build a Wall and Mexico Will Pay for It 2015)*

Prior to his speech, he declared that he had nearly $9 billion in assets, and then said:

> *"I'm really rich," Trump said while holding up a financial statement. "And that's not bragging. That's the kind of mind-set you need. We've gotta make the country rich."*

After he was elected, he said:

> *I could wait about a year and a half until we finish our negotiations with Mexico, which we'll start immediately after we get to office, but I don't want to wait (Trump, Trump: To Get Started, Mexico Will Pay for the Wall 2017)*

The Mexican president responded:

> *"At the start of the conversation with Donald Trump, I made it clear that Mexico will not pay for the wall," Mexican President Enrique Peña Nieto tweeted, after a September meeting with Trump in Mexico. (Nieto 2017)*

Because President Trump is anxious to begin work on a wall that doesn't seem to be needed any longer, I propose that the government take out a $9 billion loan in the form of bonds to get started. Those bonds would not be guaranteed by the US taxpayer. Instead, they would be guaranteed by individual investors who are confident that Mexico will pay for the wall and who are willing to put up their own assets to guarantee those bonds. The bonds would mature in 2020. If the Mexican government has not paid for the wall by that time, those assets would be sold to repay the bondholders. I suggest that President Trump and his major backers—as a show of confidence in his prediction—buy the first $9 billion.

Foreign Trade

We are experiencing a backlash against globalization of trade and manufacturing. While global trade has improved the lives of billions of people in other countries, some people in the United States have lost their jobs while others have profited greatly.

In my view, an appropriate role of government in business affairs is to set the rules of competition and then to referee the game. The rules should be fair to all the competitors, and the rulebook should be as simple as possible so everyone can understand it.

Office of Fair Business Regulations

Businesses complain about the amount of regulation as represented by an excerpt from this article in *Forbes* magazine:

> *Every one of us is probably a criminal, having violated some obscure regulation on the books of federal, state, and local municipalities at some point in our life. These regulations, once put in place, are rarely reviewed, even more rarely removed when outdated and often expanded with little notice. In 2015, the pages of the Federal Register grew by a record 81,611 pages covering 3,378 final rules and regulations, nearly 600 of which directly impact small businesses. Most of these costs are "hidden", not showing up directly in a company's books as a regulatory expense, but hidden in the cost of new and misallocated labor, materials purchased, legal costs, paperwork and the like. (Dunkelberg 2016)*

The author of that article refers to the *Federal Register*, which is a daily publication that lists both proposed and approved regulations. Once a regulation is approved, it is added to the Code of Federal Regulations (CFR). The CFR contains more than one million regulations, was 174,545 pages long in 2010, and growing by an average of a new regulation every two hours and nine minutes (Crews and Young 2013).

The sheer volume of regulations makes it easy to hide language that favors one company over another or gives a class of companies an unfair advantage, which is an invitation to corruption of public servants.

I propose that we create an Office of Fair Business Regulations (OFBR) that would perform the following:

- Review pending rules to see if they conflict with or duplicate an existing rule.
- Estimate the amount of annual labor required to meet reporting requirements.
- Estimate the cost of compliance (not counting reporting) per unit of export products, specifically for worker safety and environmental protection.
- Recommend automatic expiration (sunset) provisions if the relevance is likely to change in a few years.
- Report language that unfairly benefits a company or class of companies over their US competitors.
- Periodically review existing rules and make recommendations to Congress for repeal of those rules as a package.

The purpose of this office is to simplify the rulebook and assure that the rules of doing business in the United States are fair and not contradictory.

International Rating of Environmental and Safety Practices

Safeguarding consumer and worker health and the health of the environment is important, and complying with regulations from OSHA and the EPA can be expensive. The National Association of Manufacturers reports that federal regulations cost $2 trillion in 2012, which is 12 percent of gross domestic product and an average of about $10,000 per employee. If we require more of our companies than is required of companies in other countries, it puts US companies at a disadvantage when those costs are added to the price of their products.

I propose that we create an *Office of Regulation Equality* that evaluates the product, worker, and environmental laws and regulations of our trading partners and awards each country a rating from zero to ten where zero is comparable or better than ours and ten is the worst. The office would set tariffs on goods coming in from those countries based on the rating to offset the advantage companies in those countries would have from lower standards of product, worker, and environmental safety. Difference in wages and benefits would not be considered as part of the rating.

Chapter Thirteen
Summary of Tax Changes

Proposals for changing our federal tax laws occur in several places in this book. In this section, those ideas are reiterated so they may be considered together.

Tax-Return Voting

I propose that we make a change to our annual tax returns that are filed electronically. There would be a section that shows a pie chart representing the president's proposed budget followed by a similar pie chart showing the opposition party's budget. If a minority party like the Tea Party or the Green Party has 10 percent or more of the seats in the US House of Representatives, they could also propose a budget. Taxpayers could pick one of the proposed budgets. Each party would also propose five spending priorities that would be combined into a single list, and then taxpayers would rank the spending priorities. Taxpayers would also have the option to recommend an increase in the VAT to pay down the national debt (see Value-Added Tax (VAT)).

All recipients of income from the government due to service or automation revenue sharing must file a federal tax return and pay 5 percent of the income back to the government (see #Create a Culture of Service and Higher Education) (see #Income Inequality). Everyone should have some skin in the game and a reason to care about how the government spends "their" money.

When the tax returns are filed electronically, computers would tally the "votes" for each budget and calculate the ranking of the spending priorities. The results would be reported to the public and the Congress (see #Tax Return Voting).

Take the Profit Out of Buying Politicians

I propose that we eliminate almost all tax reductions. An exception would be tax deferments such as retirement accounts where the tax is collected at a later date and other taxes. This would reduce the corporate-tax rate from 39 percent to about 27 percent to make them more competitive with other developed countries and still collect the same amount of money. The intention of this proposal is to reduce the practice of buying politicians, the time wasted preparing tax returns, and to level the playing field for corporations to compete with each other and with foreign companies (see #End Almost All Tax Deductions and Lower the Corporate-Tax Rate).

Link Minimum Wage to CEO Income

I propose that the maximum personal federal income tax be set at 75 percent for CEOs, other top executives, and the members of their compensation committees who set CEO compensation packages that exceed one hundred times the lowest paid worker. The present top tax bracket for those earning over $415,050 is 39.6 percent. The tax would be triggered if the CEO is compensated at more than one hundred times the lowest paid wage by an employee or an employee of a contractor. In the case of part-time workers, the full-time equivalent would be used. For example, if a part-time worker is paid $9.31 an hour and works thirty hours a week for fifty-one weeks their annual pay would be $14,244. If they worked at that wage for forty hours a week, it would be $19,000. The CEO would pay a tax of 75 percent on his or her income over $1,900,000 (see #Link Minimum Wage to CEO Income Tax).

Capital-Gains Tax

Income from investments that exceed the rate of inflation would be taxed as income.

Home Sale

I propose that the government establish a table of inflation rates of housing prices by geographic region. When someone sells a house for more than he or she paid for it and he or she does not reinvest the money in another house, the table would be used to determine how much of that increase was due to inflation. Homeowners would also be able to deduct money spent on improvements while they owned the home. Because this is a primary source of savings for retirement, I would keep the deduction of $500,000 for a couple and $250,000 for a single person. The amount above either $500,000 or $250,000 after deductions for inflation and improvements would be taxed as

 Link Minimum Wage to CEO Income

income at the appropriate income tax rate (see #Income from Sale of a Residence).

Investment Property

I propose that the government establish a table of inflation rates of investment property prices by geographic region. When someone sells an investment property for more than he or she paid for it, the table would be used to determine how much of that increase was due to inflation. Property owners would also be able to deduct money spent on improvements while they owned the property. The amount after deductions for inflation and improvements would be taxed as income at the appropriate income tax rate (see #Investment Property).

Sale of Stocks

I propose that capital gain from sale of stock that has been held for more than a year be adjusted for inflation, and then if there is a net profit above the inflation, that income would be taxed at the same rate as income tax (see #Sale of Stocks).

Automation Tax

I propose that we tax profits from automation and distribute that money as a basic income to those who have completed two years of national service. The tax would be based on a ratio of profits to the number of employee hours at a rate that is intended to divert about half of the additional profits from automation to the basic income fund. Companies that use the most employees per amount of profit would pay no tax, but highly automated companies would pay up to 50 percent of the additional profits from automation. Corporate profits historically were about 5 percent, but now they are close to 10 percent of GDP while wages have fallen from 50 percent to 43 percent of GDP, which is a loss of wages of $1.26 trillion. I propose that the automation tax recover about half of that money and redistribute it to citizens who have performed two years of public service.

Value-Added Tax (VAT)

I propose that we initiate a value-added tax (VAT) to pay for balancing the budget. It would take a VAT of 11 percent to balance the budget. If congress balances the budget, the VAT would be zero unless voters choose to keep some of the tax to reduce the national debt. (see Tax-Return Voting)

Chapter Fourteen

Paying for New Programs

It's always easy to say that we should fix our problems by creating new government programs and hope to finance the additional cost through vague hopes of closing loopholes, eliminating waste, creating higher income due to greater economic activity, or reducing the size of government. In this chapter, I attempt a gross estimate of the cost of each new program and specifically identify where the money would come from to pay for them. Instead of spending the money first and hoping for additional funds to magically appear, I propose that we bring new spending programs on as the revenue or savings are realized.

Self-Funding Programs

The new programs in this group would generate income from their activities that would offset the cost of the program. They might need initial funding to get started.

Petitions, Multi-seat Districts, and Voter ID

The cost to taxpayers of primary elections is about $500 million (Gomez 2016). Instead of primaries for US or State House seats, candidates would collect petition signatures in the form of voter ID swipes. The supporters of the candidates would pay the cost of collecting signatures, and the state would use the money they would otherwise spend on primary elections to create a voter ID clearing house that would confirm signatures by those with voter IDs in real time like we do with credit-card purchases so that petitioners wouldn't have to collect extra petitions.

Militias

Militia fees would pay for maintaining internal ballistics and membership database, and the militia licensing fee would pay for the law-enforcement computer software to interface with the militia databases.

Truthfulness Ratings

News programs would subscribe to fact-checking services to check candidate statements. The cost of the service would be born by the news agency.

Prison-Population Reduction and Slum Renewal

We currently spend about $31,000 a prisoner. If we reduce our prison population by half by changing our drug laws, we could redirect the money to pay for rebuilding abandoned housing, providing construction skills and work certification to inmates, and providing them with affordable housing upon release. The slum-rebuilding program would scale up as the prison population decreases.

Electric Vehicles Powered by Sun and Wind

I own a Chevy Volt, and it is my second one. I really enjoy the experience of finding it fully charged each morning. I buy a few gallons of gasoline every month or so, but it still has the ability to drive long distances on gasoline. Presently, there is a federal tax break of about $7,000 on electric cars. I propose the elimination of all such tax breaks so that would go away. Instead, I propose that the government require the auto industry to make the batteries in the cars compatible with home electric systems so that they can take the place of a whole-house generator when the grid power fails. A typical home generator system that runs on natural gas costs about $4,000 plus installation. If your electric car could act as a home backup electric system, it would save the cost of installing a home generator and make the country more resistant to attacks on the grid by computer hackers and smooth out the variability of solar and wind generation.

The Volt is similar in size to a Chevy Malibu but costs about $10,000 more. If the number of Volts sold increases, the cost should come down a few thousand. If the price difference is only $8,000 and $4,000 of that is offset by having an auxiliary generator, $4,000 can be made up by savings on gasoline over the life of the car if you drive fifteen thousand miles a year, electricity costs $0.15 per kwh, and gasoline costs $2.50 a gallon. Europeans have taxed gasoline heavily for many years and pay about $5 a gallon compared with $2.40 in the United States.

The value of electricity varies by a factor of about three or four from nights and weekends to the workweek between 11:00 a.m. and 7:00 p.m. (Spiller 2015). If a commuter only needed half of the charge in his car to get to work and back, and he were plugged into a two-way outlet in the company's parking lot, he could program his car to sell the extra electricity during peak demand periods for three or four times what he paid for it while charging during the night. This would allow the consumer to pay the difference in cost for an electric car in about three years.

I propose making the following changes:

- Remove the taxes on gasoline of about $0.50 per gallon and shift the revenue from gasoline to annual vehicle tag license fees based on miles driven and weight. Electric vehicles should pay their share of road maintenance.
- Replace the present gasoline taxes with an adjustable tax on gasoline that makes the cost per gallon about $3.00. The tax would be adjustable to assure that alternatives to gasoline can compete against a constant price. Use the tax money to create the BusTrain mass transit system and then phase out the tax.
- Change building codes for commercial buildings to require two-way electrical connections in associated parking lots so employees could charge their cars and the company could buy electricity from their employees during peak electricity price periods.
- Use the onboard computer in an electric car to allow it to sell electricity when it is plugged in at work or away from home.

BusTrain Mass Transit
Mass transit makes sense if it is cheaper, faster, and more convenient than driving your own car. If a system is good enough to eliminate one car per household, commuters would have enough extra money each month to pay for a good transit system. The weakness of the current systems is the number of stops they make to service many people and the cost of new rights-of-way to expand rail systems. The

BusTrain system described in this book would take some development costs to design and build the busses and docking systems. The new bus systems would be much cheaper than expanding rail systems and would be paid for by the gasoline tax. The start-up costs would be paid for by a gasoline tax (see #Electric Vehicles Powered by Sun and Wind).

Border Wall with Mexico

Taxpayers should not be expected to pay for a border wall when the candidate promised us that Mexico would pay for it. Those who believe strongly in the need for such a wall are welcome to guarantee a loan to begin construction to be repaid by Mexico if their assertion proves to be correct. Otherwise, they would pay for the wall, not the US taxpayer.

Drug Research

The federal budget for research and development (R&D) is about $144 billion, $77.5 billion of which goes to the military. Of the remaining $66.5 billion, $33.6 billion is for health, $11 billion for space, $10 billion for general science, $3.55 billion for energy, $2.5 billion for natural resources and environment, and $6 billion for others (Historical Trends in Federal R&D 2017). Some of the research money currently devoted to health ($33.6 billion) could be earmarked for identifying what makes some drugs harmful or addictive and making safer recreational drugs. No additional money would be needed.

Preventative and Acute Health Care for Everyone

We are already paying for acute care in our overcrowded emergency rooms. A study in Charlotte, North Carolina, showed that out of 191,000 emergency department (ED) visits, more than half, 113,000, were for ambulatory care-sensitive conditions (ACSC) that should have been treated in a primary-care clinic. The ED visit cost three to seven times more than a visit to a primary-care clinic, which implies that about five times as many people could have been treated in a primary-care clinic for the same cost, not counting the number of people who would not have come to the clinic if they received preventative care.

Job Sharing and More Time Off
If we eliminate the idea of a paid vacation day and allow people to work less for less pay, the company will have the money they don't pay the primary employee to pay for part-time or semiretired workers at a full daily wage to increase job flexibility for employees and employers.

International Rating of Environmental and Safety Practices
I propose that we require the World Trade Organization to provide this service at no additional cost to us as a condition of our membership.

Full-Day Schools
The average money spent per student in thirty-four developed countries is $9,487 (Education at a Glance 2014 2014). The US average is $12,296 per student (Fast Facts 2013). This number implies that for a group of twenty students, we spend almost a quarter-million dollars a year ($245,920). The average teacher salary is about $57,000 plus about $19,000 (34 percent) for benefits or about $76,380 per teacher (How Much Do High School Teachers Make? 2015); (Luebke 2016). If you rented a twenty-feet-by-thirty-feet room in an office building at $20/square-foot/year, it would cost $12,000 a year. The cost of a teacher and a meeting room would be $88,380 which demonstrates that about $157,400 per class is spent on other costs and that there is an opportunity for improvement.

The average student in the United States spends 6.64 hours a day in school for 180 days per year for 1,195 hours a year (Schools and Staffing Survey 2009). This is about $10 an hour ($12,296 / 1,195 = $10.29/hr). Many working parents pay for an additional two or three hours of care before and after school at a similar rate not counting summer camp and other activities that engage students while their parents are at work (Before and After School Programs Cost 2017). If we provide an engaging school day that matches the parent's workday and work year, these costs are eliminated. If the schools are smaller and local and use Service Corps members to make it safe to walk to school (see #US Service Corps), we can reduce the cost of transportation.

Teachers already work about 10.5 hours a day during the school year for a total of 1,890 hours in a 180-day school year. If we reduce that workload to 8 hours a day but extend the school year to 217 days, the total would be 1,736 hours a year (Strauss 2012). I propose that we create a panel that compares teacher salaries to those earned by a mix of college graduates with similar degrees, grade-point averages, and experience who are working the new ten-month job schedule to determine the average teacher salary. For the sake of this exercise, let's assume this would result in an increase of 20 percent. If we reduce the other costs of education in the United States, such as transportation, to match those in other developed countries that are about 20 percent lower ($9,487 vs. $12,296), use volunteers and US Service Corps people to help with student activities, and count the extra spent on pre- and postschool care, the net cost of the program would be minimal.

Canceling Intragovernmental Loans

It's time to recognize that all those intergovernmental loans that were made from the trust funds have been spent and those are bad debts that we are carrying on the books. I propose that we declare those debts that one branch of government owes to another as null and void and that the "trust" funds are empty. This would make more people aware that we are funding our Social Security and Medicare/Medicaid payments out of annual cash flow that we exceed each year. This would decrease the official national debt by $5.34 trillion from $18.96 trillion to $13.62 trillion.

Automation Tax

I propose that we tax profits from automation and distribute that money as a basic income to those who have completed two years of national service. The tax would be based on a ratio of profits to the number of employee hours at a rate that is intended to divert about half of the additional profits from automation to the basic income fund. Companies that use the most employees per amount of profit would pay no tax, but highly automated companies would pay up to 50 percent of the additional profits from automation. The amount collected by the automation tax would be disbursed as basic income payments.

Programs That Need Funding

Let's consider approximately how much it would take to fund the programs that need additional funding and compare it to these savings and income estimates.

School of Diplomacy

The military academies run by the army, navy, and air force provide free tuition, room, and board and pay the students about $7,000 thousand a year. In 2002, the cost of each academy was between $273 million (Navy) and $365 million (Army). All three academies graduate about a thousand students a year for an average cost per graduate of $275,000 (Navy), $322,000 (Air Force) and $349,000 (Army) (Military Education 2003). Allowing for inflation, current costs would be about $400,000 per graduate.

The School of Diplomacy would cost slightly more than half as much to operate per student because the first two years of college would be completed as part of the US Service Corps or the Disaster Response Corps in which they would complete their first two years of college while working for either corps.

If the School of Diplomacy also graduated about one thousand students per year, it would cost about $200 million a year in addition to the tuition costs incurred at online schools or community colleges while participating in a service corps.

Cost: $ 0.2 billion

Disaster Response Corps

The Disaster Response Corps would use existing military infrastructure for logistics and maintenance. It would have its own heavy-lift helicopters and specialized equipment stored at air force bases that also have heavy-lift cargo planes. The size of the corps would be relatively small. A ballpark estimate of cost would be to compare it to the cost of operating a state's national guard. The

Michigan National Guard has eleven thousand members with an annual budget of $51 million (Dell 2015).

Cost: $0.051 billion

US Service Corps and Senior Service Corps
Parents of participants would be expected to pay for room and board for the two-year duration of the program. They could earn credits against this cost by housing and feeding other corps participants. For example, if the parents had a child in the program for two years, they could host (house and feed) two participants at a time for one year. The program would be administered by a core of full-time employees at the national level and by senior volunteers at the local level (see #Senior Service Corps). Participants would receive a voucher for transportation between venues as they move around the country equal to the cost of a bus or train ticket or other minimal cost option. The cost of the operation would be for the central full-time staff and bimonthly transportation around the country.

The US Service Corps and the Senior Service Corps would overlap in their missions with the AmeriCorps program, but it would be greatly expanded to include most of the young adults in the United States. The AmeriCorps budget, including funding for the Senior Corps, is about $1 billion per year employing 350,000 members or $2,857 each (Mulhere 2017). There are about thirty million Americans between the ages of eighteen to twenty-four and fifty million over sixty-two (Howden and Meyer 2011). If the young Americans spent two years in service, that would be about a third of those in that age group, or ten million. If US Service Corps and the Senior Service Corps had twelve million members, and we assume similar costs, the budget would be about $34 billion a year while the young people are in the corps.

Cost: $34 billion

Voter ID
Estimates of the number of citizens of voting age who do not have photo IDs range from sixteen to thirty-two million, and only two-

thirds of women have proof of citizenship documents that reflect their current legal name because many of them change their names when they marry (Citizens without Proof 2006). State identification cards cost about $10 for a photo ID (Non-driver State ID n.d.). Assuming that the higher number of people use the new voter ID, the cost would be $320 million if it were free. I propose charging $10 to cover the cost but waiving the charge if the applicant also attests that he or she earns less than the threshold for filing a federal tax return, which is about 45 percent of citizens, so the cost would be about $144 million (Williams 2015).

Cost: $0.144 billion

Individual Stock Funds for Retirement
We have seen that having a large amount of money in a trust fund is too much temptation for the government, so I agree with the idea that each person have an individual stock portfolio in an index fund. A stock index fund is a mutual fund comprised of representative stocks of one of the exchanges that pays dividends that match the average of a stock index such as the S&P 500 (Index Fund n.d.). Each young person would own the stock, but they could not cash it in until they retire. An exception would be made that allows each person to take out up to $500 for an emergency once every five years.

There are 1.4 million people serving in the US military (Chalabi 2015). If we assume the average enlistment of four years, that would mean that there is a turnover of about 350,000 people per year. If we assume the Disaster Relief Corps and the US Service Corps have an annual turnover of 5 million, there would be 5.35 million people each year providing service to the United States. If we awarded their service with a one-time grant of $27,000, invested in an index stock fund, the cost would be $144 billion (5.35 million × $27,000 = $144.45 billion).

Cost: $144 billion a year

Office of Fair Business Regulation
The Office of Fair Business Regulation (FBR) could be compared to the Congressional Budget Office (CBO), which has 235 staff

members (Organizing and Staffing n.d.). If we assume an annual salary of $100,000 each plus office space cost of $50 per square foot and one hundred square feet of space for half of them and the rest work remotely from home, the cost would be about $23,500,000 for salaries and $250,000 for office space for an annual budget of about $23,750,000.

Cost: $0.02375 billion

Council of Economic and Financial Advisors

The Council of Economic and Financial Advisors would cost about as much as the Supreme Court, which was $75 million for salaries and expenses plus $10 million for care of building and grounds for a total of $85 million a year (Funding/Budget - Annual Report 2015 2015).

Cost: $0.085 billion

Next-Generation Nuclear Power

China spent $300 million in five years on research to develop a prototype fail-safe molten salt reactor and is prepared to spend tens of billions of dollars to develop a commercial reactor in fifteen years (Martin 2016). I propose that we catch up with the Chinese effort before they patent most of the new technology by spending $300 million a year to develop fail-safe molten salt reactors that can use thorium or old fuel rods from conventional plants. I propose that the new research labs and prototype reactors be located in rural areas like the areas that now mine coal in Pennsylvania and West Virginia to provide new jobs as coal is displaced by cleaner energy technologies.

Cost: $0.3 billion

Universal Income

I propose that we provide job insurance to those who have completed two years of national service, including military, diplomatic service, Disaster Relief Corps, US Service Corps, and Senior Service Corps personnel. If they are laid off from a job or cannot find work, they would receive $10,000 a year. At a rate of $10,000 a year, this would support twenty-nine million people or about 9 percent of the population.

Cost: $292 billion

Balance the Budget
The budget deficit is about $443 billion per year. To balance the budget, a value added tax (VAT) would raise enough each year to make up the difference between spending and revenue. Previous attempts at increasing tax revenue by cutting taxes haven't worked.

Cost: $443 billion

Government Health Care
If the private sector fails the health-care challenge, it would be replaced by a national health-care plan similar to those in Canada, United Kingdom, and France that would cost about 10.6 percent of GDP instead of the 17.6 percent we pay now. Ten-point six percent of the $18 trillion GDP is $1.9 trillion. Present payroll and income taxes bring in $1.04 trillion.

Cost: $860 billion

Summary of Needed Funding
The programs that need funding in billion dollars ($):

School of Diplomacy	0.2
Disaster Relief Corps	0.051
US Service and Senior Corps	34
Voter ID	0.144
Individual Stock Retirement fund	144
Office of Fair Business Regulation	0.02375
Council of Economic Advisors	0.085
Safe Nuclear Power Research	0.3
Universal Income	292
Balance the Budget	443
Government Health Care	<u>860</u>
Total	1,774

Income Generating or Savings Programs
The ideas in this section either generate income or reduce costs so that money can be available for other new programs.

End Tax Deductions and Lower Tax Rates
Each year we play this game with the government where we start with an amount we owe in taxes and then try to add up as many deductions as we can to lower that amount. After spending a day or two on our tax return, I end up paying about the same percentage that I did last year, and I invariably cry out, "Why don't we just tax everyone at the lower rate and cut out all this work!"

For example, the tax bracket for those earning between $38,000 and $92,000 is 25% but the effective rate after deductions is less than 15% for most of them (Effective Tax Rate by Size of Income 2017).

The US tax code has seventy thousand pages of instructions for filing tax returns. Each year about 169 million individual Americans file tax returns after spending an average of 8 hours and paying an average of $120 for assistance for a total of 1.35 billion hours and $20 billion. US businesses file ten million returns spending about $420 for assistance and 23 hours of preparation time for a total of 240 million hours and $4.4 billion (McCaherty 2014). Together the cost of preparing our taxes is about $24.4 billion and 1.59 billion hours. If we eliminate all the tax deductions except for deferred income like IRAs, we could easily save half of the money we are now spending on tax-preparation services. I propose that we eliminate tax deductions except for deferred income and lower the tax rate on corporations from 39 percent to the effective rate they are actually paying (27 percent) and on personal income to 15%. One percentage point of corporate tax raises about $10 billion (Key Elements of the U.S. Tax System 2016). I propose that we add back a tax of 2.2 percent to the effective tax rate to recoup 12.2 billion which is half the tax preparation cost for use on other projects. The corporate tax rate would be reduced from 39% to 29.2% and the personal tax bracket from 25% to 17.2% but without most deductions.

Income: $12.2 billion annually

Sale of Legalized Drugs

The federal government makes about $9.7 billion a year by taxing the sale of alcohol (Options for Reducing the Deficit: 2014 to 2023 2013). If we legalize marijuana nationwide, it would increase federal income by about $7 billion a year (Ekins and Henchman 2016).

Income: $7 billion annually

Habituating drugs that provide a large portion of criminal profits like cocaine ($28 billion), heroin ($27 billion), and meth ($13 billion) would be more closely managed. Habitual users of these drugs spend more than most people can legally afford, which contributes to crime. I propose that these drugs not only be sold in government-operated outlets where the price is much lower than illegal sources to deny those profits to organized crime but also monitored with free addiction counseling. If the government sells these drugs for 10 percent of their present street price, it would make the addiction more affordable for the addicts but still bring in about $6.8 billion to the government.

Income: $6.8 billion annually

Audit of the Department of Defense

Fiscal conservatives pride themselves with being better money managers than their liberal counterparts and often refer to reducing government waste as a source of money for other projects or for tax cuts. Since spending on Social Security, Medicare, and Medicaid comprises more than half the budget, it would seem reasonable that those categories would be the first place to look for potential savings by eliminating waste (Jacobson 2015).

In the Chief Financial Officers Act of 1990, the Congress found the following:

1. *General management functions of the Office of Management and Budget need to be significantly enhanced to improve the efficiency and effectiveness of the Federal Government.*

2. *Financial management functions of the Office of Management and Budget need to be significantly enhanced to provide overall direction and leadership in the development of a modern Federal financial management structure and associated systems.*

3. *Billions of dollars are lost each year through fraud, waste, abuse, and mismanagement among the hundreds of programs in the Federal Government.*

4. *These losses could be significantly decreased by improved management, including improved central coordination of internal controls and financial accounting.*

5. *The Federal Government is in great need of fundamental reform in financial management requirements and practices as financial management systems are obsolete and inefficient, and do not provide complete, consistent, reliable, and timely information.*

6. *Current financial reporting practices of the Federal Government do not accurately disclose the current and probable future cost of operating and investment decisions, including the future need for cash or other, resources, do not permit adequate comparison of actual costs among executive agencies, and do not provide the timely information required for efficient management of programs. (Chief Financial Officers Act of 1990 1990)*

The place to start an investigation of waste is to examine the annual audit of how the money allocated by Congress was spent. One can conduct such an examination of the agencies that administer Social Security, Medicare, and Medicaid because they publish an audit that meets the requirements of Congress (The Office of Audit n.d.). The Department of Defense does not keep track of how it spends US tax dollars well enough to pass an audit.

Since the end of World War II, war has been in an overall decline. The global death rate fell from 22 per 100,000 in 1945 to 1.4 in 2014 (Goldstein and Pinker 2016). The US military has provided the world with a strong defender against expansionist regimes like the Soviet Union and Iraq and helped maintain peace. We saw the advantage of investing in military R&D when our modern tanks and airplanes fought in the Gulf War and defeated Soviet-era equipment with few losses. The cost of providing this world peacekeeping force is about 16 percent of the US budget (Jacobson 2015). The military budget was $597 billion in 2016 or $1,842 per US citizen ($7,368 per family of four), is about a third of world military spending, and almost as much as the next fourteen countries combined (Taylor and Karklis 2016).

In 2015, a report showed that there was a total of $6.5 trillion of adjustments in the 2015 army budget out of only $587 billion for the entire military. This implies that for every dollar Congress allocated for military spending in 2015, there were at least $10 of "adjustments" (Paltrow 2016). A bi-partisan bill was introduced to require the Department of Defense to update its accounting methods to make them auditable by 2017. None of the military branches have met preliminary targets for making their books auditable, and at this time they are expected to fail to meet the 2017 deadline (Serbu 2017).

I propose that we mandate a 10 percent cut in the Department of Defense budget if they fail to meet the 2017 deadline for becoming auditable. Once the budgets of the armed forces become available for analysis, it is highly likely that at least 10 percent could be identified as waste or fraud freeing up $59 billion. Once the DOD issues an auditable accounting of how much money they spend and where it comes from, we will have a better idea of where the $5 trillion in trust-fund money have gone. If almost all of the $5 trillion have been spent by the DOD, it would take almost half of their annual budget to repay that money in twenty years, which would be more than most people would support.

I propose that we expect the DOD to improve the management of its present budget enough to eliminate 10 percent due to waste, fraud, and mismanagement. In addition, in exchange for cancelling its intergovernmental debt, I propose that we set a spending goal that is relevant to that spent by our most likely adversaries. For example, we could spend one and a half as much as Russia and China combined, which would be $450 billion or a reduction of $150 billion, $59 billion of which would be savings from improved management.

Income: $150 billion

CEO Tax on Income Greater than 100× Minimum Wage
If the average CEO of a S&P 500 company makes $10 million and if the minimum wage is about $14,500 ($7.50/hr × 40 hr/wk × 50 weeks) and we tax the excess beyond 100× at an additional 35 percent, the income from the tax on those five hundred CEOs would be: ($10,000,000 − 100 × $14,500) × 35% × 500 = $1.5 billion. The intent would be to encourage companies to raise the minimum wage to eventually make this source of income go away by increasing the minimum wage.

Income: $1.5 billion

Tax Capital Gains as Income
Only 13 percent of taxpayers pay capital-gains taxes, and they are in the higher tax brackets of 33 percent to 39 percent, and only 0.1 percent of people inherit stock in trust funds without paying capital gains on the stock's increase prior to the inheritance (Kolawole 2008); (Mufson 2015). The IRS estimates that about 9.2 percent of individual tax revenue is from capital gains (Merritt 2010). Individual income tax revenue is about $1.6 trillion which means that income from capital-gains tax is about $147 billion ($1.6 trillion × 9.2 percent) (Amount of Revenue by Source 2017). If capital gains are taxed as income at 35 percent instead of 20 percent, the additional income would be about $109 billion.

Income: $109 billion

Automation Tax

I propose a tax on profits from automation that is based on the ratio of wages to corporate profits. If wages and employee profit-sharing plans amount to less than 50 percent of a company's expenses and its profits after taxes are greater than 5 percent, the profits above 5 percent after other taxes would be taxed at a rate of 50 percent.

If about half of the $1.26 trillion that have been diverted from wages is recovered by this tax, the income would be $63 billion.

Income: $63 billion

Balance the Budget

I propose that we institute a value-added tax (VAT) of about 11 percent or 12 percent. The amount of the VAT would be tied to our spending. If we decide to send more troops into another country or pay for hurricane relief, the extra spending would be paid for the next year by an increase in the VAT. Conversely, if the Congress acts to reduce spending, the VAT would go down.

Income: $443 billion

Health-Care Challenge: Reduced Costs by 40 Percent

The gross domestic product (GDP) of the United States is about $18 trillion (GDP (current US$) 2016). One percent of GDP is $180 billion. If the health-care system in the United States meets the health-care challenge and reduces its costs by 1 percent of GDP per year for seven years to bring our costs down from 17.6 percent of GDP to 10.6 percent to match the spending level of other developed countries, the savings would be as follows in each year:

- Year one: $180 billion
- Year two: $360 billion
- Year three: $540 billion
- Year four: $720 billion
- Year five: $900 billion
- Year six: $1.08 trillion
- Year seven: $1.26 trillion

The federal budget for Medicare and Medicaid in 2016 was $788 billion or 4.4 percent of GDP, which implies that the rest of the 17.6 percent of GDP health-care costs, 13.2 percent of GDP, are paid for by employers and employees. If the cost of health care is reduced to 10.6 percent to match other countries, employers and employees would only have to pay 6.2 percent (the difference between 4.4 percent and 10.6 percent) of GDP instead of 13.2 percent for a net savings to employers and employees of 7 percent of GDP or $1.26 trillion. If this savings translates into increased wages by employees and increased profits by corporations and it is taxed at an average rate of 20 percent, the increase in tax revenue to the government would be $250 billion.

Income: $250 billion

Health-Care Challenge: Government Health Care
If the private sector fails the health-care challenge, it would be replaced by a national health-care plan similar to those in Canada, United Kingdom, and France that would cost about 10.6 percent of GDP instead of the 17.6 percent we pay now. Ten-point six percent of the $18 trillion GDP is $1.9 trillion.

I propose that we raise the $1.9 trillion using the following methods:

1. Keep the present Medicare payroll tax of 2.9 percent and other taxes that pay for the government's present share of health care in the form of Medicare and Medicaid, which totals $1.04 trillion.
2. Convert employer medical-insurance payments into increases in wages of about $13,000 per family. Employees would not have to pay $5,000 for their share of the medical-insurance premium, which would remove this tax deduction and increase their total taxable income by $18,000.
3. Rename the Medicare payroll tax as the Health Care payroll tax. The present Medicare payroll tax is 2.9 percent shared equally between employees and employers that brings in $234 billion (Key Elements of the U.S. Tax System 2017). The new

Health Care tax would be an additional 10.66 percent on employees to raise the remaining $0.86 trillion.

If the median household makes $56,500 and $13,000 is added to that, the new median income would be $69,500. If the Health Care Payroll Tax (HCPT) is increased by 10.66 percent, the household would pay $7,410 more in HCPT.

The employees would not have to pay $5,000 for their share of the health-care premiums, which is tax deductible, so they would have $5,000 more taxable income. The taxable household income would increase by a net of $10,590 ($13,000 + $5,000 − $7,410). If they pay 20 percent income tax, the amount of income tax they pay would increase by $2,120.

There are about ninety-three million households that pay federal taxes (45 Percent of Americans Pay No Federal Income Tax 2016). At $2,120 per household, there would be a net increase in income-tax revenue of $197 billion.

Summary of Savings and Increased Income

A summary of savings and income options is as follows:

The savings and income proposals in billion dollars ($):

- End tax deductions, lower tax rate, share savings — 12.2
- Sale of marijuana — 7
- Restricted sale of cocaine, heroin, and meth — 6.8
- Audit DOD, 10 percent savings and reduce to 1.5× Russia plus China — 150
- CEO tax on income 100× minimum wage — 1.5
- Capital-gains taxes on unearned income — 51
- Automation tax — 63
- Balance the budget with a VAT — 443
- Government Health Care payroll tax — 860
- Increase income tax from employer pay increase — 197
- Total — $1,791 billion

This is a rough estimate, but it shows that the proposals that need $1,770 billion can be paid for with $1,791 billion of increased revenue and savings. The difference could be applied to the national debt.

Here is a summary of what these changes cost the average tax-paying household:

- Payment of employer's share of health care as wages: +$13,000
- Nonpayment of employee's share of health insurance: +$5,000
- New health-care payroll tax: −$7,410
- Income tax of 20 percent on additional taxable income: −$2,120
- VAT to balance the budget: −$3,000
- Most households would not be affected by proposed changes in capital-gains taxes or measures designed to reduce income inequality.

The effect of these proposals on most households would be:
Reduce health care cost by 40 percent: $8,470
Balanced budget value-added tax: −$3,000
                        Increase family income $5,470

Chapter Fifteen

How to Begin

The Beckhard-Harris Change Model describes three conditions that are necessary for change to overcome resistance (Gleicher, Beckhard and Harris 1987):

- Dissatisfaction
- Clear, shared vision of a preferred future
- Acceptable first steps

I would add that to be acceptable, the first steps must seem possible and affordable. The first thirteen chapters in this book deal with topics where the dissatisfaction is assumed and they focus on creating a shared and preferred vision for the future. In the previous chapter, the subject of affordability was discussed. In this final chapter, we consider what first steps can be taken that are acceptable and possible and methods of overcoming resistance.

Personal Beginnings

One response I get from people who have read the book is "You should run for office!" This statement reminds me of President Kennedy's speech in which he said, "[A]sk not what your country can do for you—ask what you can do for your country." I've taken eleven months to write this book. I ask each of you to consider what you can do. Here are some suggestions:

Throw the Flag

Years ago, I was having a discussion with my wife, and I frequently used the terms *liberal* and *conservative*. My wife said she didn't know what I meant by those terms and asked me to look them up. They are (Merriam-Webster n.d.):

- *Liberal: broad-minded; especially: not bound by authoritarianism, orthodoxy, or traditional forms*
- *Conservative: tending or disposed to maintain existing views, conditions, or institutions*

At the time, Democrats controlled both houses of Congress and the presidency. I suggested assuming the Democrats wanted to maintain the existing balance of power that they must be conservatives. Today, I observe that many people who consider themselves liberals are devoted to avoiding climate change, which would make them climate conservatives. It's no wonder that we have difficulty communicating about politics.

Another example of the importance of the meaning of words is *cut*. If we look up the word in *Merriam-Webster*, the meaning is:

Cut: to reduce in amount

When discussing funding for programs in the future that are projected to increase in cost, many people use the word *cut* if the increase in funding is less than the anticipated increase in cost. One may argue that increasing funding for Medicaid by 20 percent when the projected cost increase is 50 percent results in a reduction, but calling it a cut diverts the discussion from the real issue—runaway cost increases (Gillin 2017).

We need to engage with those with whom we disagree, and I suggest that the way to begin is to lay some ground rules for a civil discussion. First, we need to agree that the possibility exists that the other person might be right or have a better idea. This begins with our own view. Second, we need to agree on authorities to which we can appeal when we differ about the facts of a situation (see #Throw the Flag). For example, I used the *Merriam-Webster* dictionary as my source for the definitions of *liberal, conservative*, and *cut*.

Checking the facts of stories is more important than ever, especially since it has been revealed that the Russians intentionally spread false stories during political campaigns (Reston 2017). There are several websites that review the accuracy of political statements and Internet rumors such as Politifact.com, FactCheck.org, OpenSecrets.org, Snopes.com, TruthOrFiction.com, and Hoax-Slayer.com (Vikram n.d.). With an agreement on how to assure that our conversations are based on reliable facts, more productive discussions are possible.

Here are some of the guidelines and steps from WikiHow that has a quarter-million views for getting involved in local politics (WikiHow to Get Involved in Local Politics n.d.):

- Be a poll watcher.
- Participate in voting-place party meetings.
- Help with local vote counting.
- Become a better speaker by practicing on small groups.
- Register voters and canvass neighborhoods in support of a position.
- Avoid making impossible promises.
- Live by what you say you believe.

Every Vote Counts in Local Elections

Changing our election process begins by using a different method to elect representatives in small venues such as library boards, church boards, and city council where the method of electing officials can be decided locally. People need a chance to become familiar with a new method and test its benefits and expose its weaknesses (see #Replace Winner-Take-All Elections).

Reading Volunteers

Some schools already have programs that allow adults to volunteer as tutors, and there are websites that serve to connect volunteers with schools like ReadingPartners (Volunteer 2017).

Recognize Diplomatic and Domestic Service

It is commonplace at baseball and football games to recognize the service by our military personnel. If you have an opportunity, you can suggest that we include those who have served in the diplomatic corps, the Peace Corps, Vista, or Volunteers for America to raise public awareness of an alternative to military service and to honor peacemaking and community service equally with military service.

Electric Vehicles

I leased a Chevy Volt in 2013 and drove it for three years. The Volt is primarily an electric car with a range of thirty-five to fifty miles, but it also has a gasoline engine with a small tank and a range of three hundred miles. It is well engineered, and I loved it. The Volt is about the same size as a Chevy Malibu, an all-gasoline car. The Volt sells for a premium at $42,000, and the government provides a $7,000 rebate, which brings it down to $35,000. The Malibu sells for about $22,000. At $4 a gallon for gasoline, I calculated that the savings on gasoline would eventually make up the difference. Now that gasoline is under $3 a gallon, the savings on gasoline versus electricity from the utility cannot make up that difference in initial price even though I averaged over two hundred miles per gallon with the Volt.

When my lease was up in 2016, I found that the lease buyout price was much higher than the market price of a used Volt. Now the difference in price between a 2013 Volt and a 2013 Malibu is only about $2,000 (2013 Chevrolet Volt for Sale 2017). Last year, I bought a used Volt with thirty-six thousand miles on it for $16,000, and I plan to drive it for another six or seven years. The battery has a one hundred thousand–mile warranty. If you drive less than thirty-five miles a day most of the time and want to eliminate air pollution from your car, check out a used Chevy Volt.

If you are building a house in a sunny climate, consider using Elon Musk's photocell shingles, a Powerwall battery, and a Tesla automobile (Solar Roof 2017).

Graceful Exit

As a member of the baby-boom generation, I'm accustomed to seeing the American culture adapt to my generation's needs and desires. I watched my father die an uncomfortable and sometimes painful death, and he was paying $10,000 a month for nursing care near the end. I vowed that I would not end my days in that manner and that I'd rather have my assets pass on to my children and grandchildren instead of paying for expensive care and surgery to prolong my life by one or two more years. I like the idea of making a graceful exit from life that is voluntary and that supports the emotional needs of those who love me, and I expect that many other baby boomers share those sentiments.

If you have similar goals, here are some suggestions:

- Make a living will with health directives that make your decisions clear (Download Your State's Advanced Directives 2016).
- Contact groups like Final Exit Network and Compassion and Choices that provide information about voluntarily terminating your own life and see what they can provide. (Compassion & Choices n.d.); (Supporting the Human Right to Death with Dignity 2017).
- Talk with your religious leaders about having a celebration of life service instead of a funeral.

If you do not share this view, I respect your choice. I just ask that people respect each other's choice in this very personal matter.

State Politics

States have jurisdiction over implementation of several of the big ideas described in this book. If your state legislature does not represent the will of the majority of voters in your state, you can bypass the legislature and take the vote directly to the voters if you live in one of the twenty-six states that have this provision. The states that have provisions that allow voters to vote on issues directly are:

Alaska, Arizona, Arkansas, California, Colorado, Florida, Idaho, Illinois, Maine, Maryland, Massachusetts, Michigan, Mississippi, Missouri, Montana, Nebraska, New Mexico, Nevada, North Dakota, Ohio, Oklahoma, Oregon, South Dakota, Utah, Washington, and Wyoming

(States with Initiative or Referendum 2017)

Amend State Constitutions to Change State Voting Laws

One of the major roadblocks to changing our voting laws is the self-interest of those who are current office holders who got elected under the present system. Because it worked for them, they would be unlikely to approve a change. Fortunately, many states allow voters to place initiatives directly on the ballot without approval of established officials. Eighteen states allow voters to amend the state's constitution by direct ballot to allow for a different voting system (see #Replace Winner-Take-All Elections). They are:

> Arizona, Arkansas, California, Colorado, Florida, Illinois, Massachusetts, Michigan, Mississippi, Missouri, Montana, Nebraska, Nevada, North Dakota, Ohio, Oklahoma, Oregon, and South Dakota

If you live in one of these eighteen states, you can work to allow voters to change the way your state elects its House of Representatives and replace the primary, winner-take-all method and its gerrymandered districts with the multi-candidate system (see Replace Winner-Take-All Elections).

State Initiatives

In the twenty-six states that allow voter initiatives by direct ballot, you can work to gather signatures to place new laws described in this book directly before the public on the following issues:

- License local militias to regulate the ownership of guns.
- Reform education to help students to mature.
- Reform prisons and rebuild slums.
- Create a BusTrain mass transit system.
- Require utilities to match increases in solar and wind with storage.
- Divert profits from sale of drugs from criminals to state programs.
- Allow people to choose to end their own lives on their own terms.

National Reforms: Big Ideas to Campaign for Change

Some changes must be made at the national level. To accomplish these goals, candidates must run for office who have new, big ideas that excite enough voter support to overcome the established power structure. The topics that I would suggest to candidates for national office would be:

Automation Value Sharing

There is a big opportunity to get out in front of this issue with 2.5 million middle-class, mostly white voters who are truck drivers. The technology to replace their jobs is already here and will be rolled out in the next few years. The candidate who has a plan to share the benefits of automation with those workers will have an appreciative audience.

Culture of Service Combined with Benefits

The people who pay taxes often resent the idea that their tax money is given to people who do not pay taxes. However, when we meet someone who served in the military, it is commonplace to thank them for their service because we appreciate what they have done for the country, and it is a scandal that those veterans do not get prompt medical attention or that there are thirty-nine thousand homeless veterans (Bronstein, Black and Griffin 2014); (FAQ about homeless veterans n.d.).

I suggest that a candidate could link national service with government benefits. National service would include military personnel but be expanded to include most of our young people who participate in the US Service Corps and Disaster Relief Corps. The candidate could propose that we replace entitlements with benefits for national service. We must end the disgrace of homeless veterans begging on our streets.

The Health-Care Challenge

The ideas about health care that are currently being debated are capping the increase in health-care costs or continuing to pay more each year. Neither group addresses the real problem, which is runaway costs. The simple fact about health care in the United States is that we are paying almost twice as much as other countries that provide health care to all their citizens. The money we waste on our present system could fund many programs of much greater benefit. The health-care challenge gives private corporations a chance to prove that they can do better than government. If not, we switch to national health care and spend part of the difference on funding other programs and the rest on relieving business from this burden.

Take the Profit and Corruption Out of Drug Sales

Let's back candidates who call a cease-fire on the war on drugs and remove the economic benefits of buying elected officials. Conservatives who often champion states' rights are trying to oppose the rights of states to legalize marijuana. Call on conservatives to respect states' rights if that has been part of their past campaign rhetoric. Legalization is popular and reflects a more rational approach to recreational drug use.

Take the Profit Out of Buying Congresspersons

A candidate could run on a platform of reforming Congress by reforming the tax code to reduce the benefit to corporations of buying politicians and cutting tax rates for corporations to competitive levels. Approval rating of Congress is at 20 percent as of April 2017 (Norman 2017).

Voter Registration and Participation

Voter registration is often viewed as a ploy to suppress the vote of the poor and minorities in the name of preventing voter fraud. I have found that the sin someone sees in another is the sin with which he or she is most familiar. My concern is that those who are claiming that millions of people voted illegally in 2016 without proof are themselves considering it (Fact-check: Did 3 million Undocumented Immigrants Vote in this Year's Election? 2016). A candidate could perform a jujitsu move on this issue. Conservatives have been opposed to national ID cards in the past, but now is the time to push for them but use the method in this book to enroll even more citizens rather than fewer (Nowrasteh 2010) (see #Voter ID).

Gun Laws Supporting Local Militias

We have been deadlocked on the issue of responsible and legal gun ownership despite a large majority of voters favoring simple measures such as background checks of all gun sales, including private gun sales at gun shows (Selby 2015). A candidate can run on a platform of supporting the Second Amendment right to bear arms and appeal to most people who are in favor of sensible regulation by supporting a measure to license local militias whose members would be responsible for each other (see #License Small Militias).

Revise Citizenship and Immigration laws
Another core conservative issue is protection of the country from unregulated immigration. This issue can be resolved without deporting millions of hardworking immigrants while restoring control of immigration. Since 40 percent of the people who are here illegally arrived legally but overstayed their visit, we should address that issue first. This issue combines with a national voter ID with a biometric that would work with a national database to confirm that people leave when they are supposed to.

There is a trade-off between conservatives and liberals on the issue of citizenship. For the conservatives, the candidate can suggest that we revise the law so that birth by a US citizen conveys citizenship rather than birth on US soil. For liberals, those who have lived here illegally for a certain minimum number of years or who have children who are citizens can become legal by serving for two years. The service could be done by relatives who are citizens if the people are older adults who could not leave their jobs. This proposal would appeal to ethnic minorities who are already voters.

Revise Taxes
We need to recognize that productivity by our businesses is the source of the money that we want to spend on benefits programs and that the tax environment should relieve corporations of the burden of paying for health care, lobbyists, and donations to elected officials to get tax breaks and complying with a byzantine tax code while requiring them to share the wealth of automation and corporate profits with the public. The tax proposals in this book provide a large net benefit to corporations, many of which would support a candidate who ran on this platform.

Safe Nuclear Power Research
We need a long-range plan for clean energy that also provides jobs for Americans. Advocates of solar and wind power assume that manufacturing solar panels and wind turbines will create jobs in the United States, but like other forms of manufacturing, these devices

can be made cheaper in China, and Chinese subsidies can bankrupt competing manufacturers (Bradsher 2017).

Wind turbines rely on ultra-strong magnets that are made of steel with added rare-earth metals such as neodymium. China supplies 85 percent of the world's rare-earth metals, including those needed to make wind turbines (Bushong 2013). China was forced by the World Trade Organization (WTO) to end its practice of limiting export of rare-earth metals in 2015, but it still has the advantage of using its own resources to manufacture wind turbines and the threat to investors in US companies that it could cut off supplies (China Drops Its Export Limits on Rare Earths 2015).

The United States is a world leader in high-tech manufacturing, and we need a program that creates clean energy jobs in the United States that not only provide clean energy for our country but also provide an export to developing countries.

A candidate could appeal to the thirty-three-thousand coal miners who lost their jobs since 2012 by declaring a new Manhattan Project (Jeffrey 2016). The Manhattan Project created 130,000 jobs, many of which were in central Tennessee and rural Washington State during World War II (Manhattan Project 2012). We could build the research, manufacturing, and installation of new, safe nuclear plants in areas of the country that are economically impacted by a shift to clean energy and whose voters will realize by the next election that coal-mining jobs are not coming back.

Overcoming Resistance

Most of us are conservatives when it comes to change, and our first response to a proposal for change is resistance even if we are dissatisfied with the current situation. There are three methods that are helpful in overcoming resistance (Gibb 2016):

- Go with the resistance, but redirect it.
- Imagine a win-win; listen to understand and then be understood and synergize.

- Embrace the resistance, identify concerns, and incorporate suggestions.

Overcoming Resistance

Final Comment

A friend of mine once told me that the people he met from other countries share the impression that the United States is essentially an optimistic place. I have enjoyed the process of writing this book because it has focused my mind on an optimistic vision for our country. If you share that optimism, or would like to, I suggest that you share this book with your friends and talk about this vision for America and how we can make it a reality by encouraging our best people to run for office and to support big ideas like those described above for our shared future.

The Kindle version of the book contains active hyperlinks between sections of the book and from the Works Cited directly to the websites from which the references were taken to facilitate your own discovery and the ability to check the accuracy and possible bias of the sources I used. You might consider using this book for a discussion group and encourage people to use the hyperlinks to expand their knowledge of each of these subjects in order to make a fuller contribution to the discussion.

John Preston

Links to Works Cited

About the National Transportation Safety Board. 2017. https://www.ntsb.gov/about/Pages/default.aspx.

Albert Einstein's Quote. n.d. http://www.myanmars.net/myanmar-history/albert-einstein-quote.htm.

Alexander, Michelle. 2010. *The New Jim Crowe.* The New Press.

Alonso-Zaldivar, Ricardo. 2016. "$10,345 Per Person: U.S. Health Care Spending Reaches New Peak." July 13. http://www.pbs.org/newshour/rundown/new-peak-us-health-care-spending-10345-per-person/.

Alton, Larry. 2016. "What Will Happen When AI Starts Replacing White-Collar Jobs?" March 25. https://www.forbes.com/sites/larryalton/2016/05/25/what-will-happen-when-ai-starts-replacing-white-collar-jobs/#20dc387e1639.

Amount of Revenue by Source. 2017, February 15. http://www.taxpolicycenter.org/statistics/amount-revenue-source.

Andrabi, Tahir, and Jishnu Das. 2010. "In Aid We Trust: Hearts and Minds and the Pakistan Earthquake of 2005." September. http://www.belfercenter.org/sites/default/files/legacy/files/uploads/mei/conference/andrabi-inaidwetrust.pdf.

Annual Cost to Own and Operate a Vehicle Falls to $8,798, Finds AAA. 2015. http://newsroom.aaa.com/2015/04/annual-cost-operate-vehicle-falls-8698-finds-aaa-archive/.

Anwar, Andre. 2007. "Prostitution Ban Huge Success in Sweden." November 8. http://www.spiegel.de/international/europe/criminalizing-the-customers-prostitution-ban-huge-success-in-sweden-a-516030.html.

Any Anxiety Disorder among Children. n.d. https://www.nimh.nih.gov/health/statistics/prevalence/any-anxiety-disorder-among-children.shtml.

Background on Commission. 2014.
http://wedrawthelines.ca.gov/commission.html.

Barro, Josh. 2012. "Is It True That Only 85 Million Americans Pay
Federal Tax? No." April 17.
https://www.forbes.com/sites/joshbarro/2012/04/17/everything-about-this-drudge-headline-is-wrong/#360dd9b927b2.

Beaumont Health First in Michigan to Treat Cancer Patient with Protons.
2017, July 13. https://www.beaumont.org/health-wellness/press-releases/beaumont-health-first-in-michigan-to-treat-cancer-patient-with-protons.

Before and After School Programs Cost. 2017.
http://education.costhelper.com/before-and-after-school-care.html.

Bellis, Mary. n.d. "History of the Wheelchair."
http://inventors.about.com/od/famousinventions/fl/Textile-Industry-and-Textile-Machinery-of-the-Industrial-Revolution.htm.

Bernstein, Lenny. 2016. "U.S. Life Expectancy Declines for the First
Time since 1993." December 8.
https://www.washingtonpost.com/national/health-science/us-life-expectancy-declines-for-the-first-time-since-1993/2016/12/07/7dcdc7b4-bc93-11e6-91ee-1adddfe36cbe_story.html.

Best, Jo. 2016. "IBM Watson: The Inside Story of How the Jeopardy-Winning Supercomputer Was Born, and What It Wants to
Do Next " http://www.techrepublic.com/article/ibm-watson-the-inside-story-of-how-the-jeopardy-winning-supercomputer-was-born-and-what-it-wants-to-do-next/.

Best Jobs: High School Teacher. 2015.
http://money.usnews.com/careers/best-jobs/high-school-teacher/salary.

Biello, David. 2007. "Back to the Future: How the Brain "Sees" the
Future." January 2.
https://www.scientificamerican.com/article/back-to-the-future-how-th/.

Bihari, Michael. 2016. "Learn about Insurance Codes to Avoid Billing Errors." August 19. https://www.verywell.com/learn-about-insurance-codes-to-avoid-billing-errors-1738628.

Bjerga, Alan. 2015. "The Great Plains' Looming Water Crisis." July 2. https://www.bloomberg.com/news/articles/2015-07-02/great-plains-water-crisis-aquifer-s-depletion-threatens-farmland.

Blakinger, Keri. 2016. "A Look at Some of the Ways George Orwell's "1984" Has Come True Today." June 6. http://www.nydailynews.com/news/national/ways-george-orwell-1984-true-article-1.2662813.

Bond, Casey. 2014. "One in Five Americans Know Where Their Income Tax Dollars Go." March 17. https://www.gobankingrates.com/personal-finance/federal-income-tax-receipt/.

Bradner, Eric. 2017. "McConnell: No Federal Money Should Be Spent on Trump's Voter Fraud Investigation." February 5. http://www.cnn.com/2017/02/05/politics/mitch-mcconnell-voter-fraud-states-trump/.

Bradsher, Keith. 2017. "When Solar Panels Became Job Killers." April 8. https://www.nytimes.com/2017/04/08/business/china-trade-solar-panels.html.

Breeze, David. n.d. "History of Hadrian's Wall." http://www.english-heritage.org.uk/visit/places/hadrians-wall/history/.

Bronstein, Scott, Nelli Black, and Drew Griffin. 2014. "Veterans Dying Because of Health Care Delays." January 30. http://www.cnn.com/2014/01/30/health/veterans-dying-health-care-delays/index.html.

Budget: Research for the People. 2017, March 6. https://www.nih.gov/about-nih/what-we-do/budget.

Bushong, Steven. 2013. "Rare Earths, Minerals Used in Windpower Technology, Could Fall into Short Supply." June 4. http://www.windpowerengineering.com/uncategorized/rare-earths-minerals-used-in-windpower-technology-could-fall-into-short-supply/.

Links to Works Cited

Cancer Statistics. 2016. https://www.cancer.gov/about-cancer/understanding/statistics.

Capital Gain. n.d. http://www.investopedia.com/terms/c/capitalgain.asp.

Carroll, Joseph. 2005. "Greatest U.S. President? Public Names Reagan, Clinton, Lincoln." February 10. http://www.gallup.com/poll/14974/greatest-us-president-public-names-reagan-clinton-lincoln.aspx.

Cavendish, Richard. 2015. "The Great Conqueror Took the Chinese City on June 1st, 1215." June 6. http://www.historytoday.com/richard-cavendish/genghis-khan-takes-beijing.

The Center for Research on Population and Security. 1993. "Index of Issues." January. Accessed February 21, 2011. http://www.population-security.org/mumf-93-01.htm.

Chalabi, Mona. 2015. "What Percentage of Americans Have Served in the Military." March 19. https://fivethirtyeight.com/datalab/what-percentage-of-americans-have-served-in-the-military/.

Chamberlain, Dr. Andrew. 2015. "CEO to Worker Pay Ratios: Average CEO Earns 204 Times Median Worker Pay." August 25. https://www.glassdoor.com/research/ceo-pay-ratio/.

Chief Financial Officers Act of 1990. 1990. http://govinfo.library.unt.edu/npr/library/misc/cfo.html.

China Drops Its Export Limits on Rare Earths. 2015, January 5. https://www.nytimes.com/2015/01/06/business/international/china-drops-its-export-limits-on-rare-earths.html.

Cho, Ardian. 2012. "Once Again, Physicists Debunk Faster-than-Light Neutrinos." June 8. http://www.sciencemag.org/news/2012/06/once-again-physicists-debunk-faster-light-neutrinos.

Cho, Seo-Young, Axel Dreher, and Eric Neumayer. 2013. "Does Legalized Prostitution Increase Human Trafficking?" *World Development* 41: 67–82.

Citizens United v. Federal Election Commission. 2009, October. https://www.supremecourt.gov/opinions/09pdf/08-205.pdf.

Citizens without Proof. 2006, November. http://www.brennancenter.org/sites/default/files/legacy/d/downloa d_file_39242.pdf.

CMS Fast Fact. 2017, April 11. https://www.cms.gov/research-statistics-data-and-systems/statistics-trends-and-reports/cms-fast-facts/index.html.

Cohn, D'Vera. 2013. "Data Show a Dent in American's Love for Cars." July 1. http://www.pewresearch.org/fact-tank/2013/07/01/data-show-a-dent-in-americans-love-for-cars/.

Colley, David P. 2003. *Blood for Dignity: The Story of the First Integrated Combat Unit in the U.S. army.* New York: St. Martin.

Crews, Wayne, and Ryan Young. 2013. "Twenty Years of Non-Stop Regulation." June 5. https://spectator.org/55475_twenty-years-non-stop-regulation/.

Definition of Insurance. 2017. https://www.merriam-webster.com/dictionary/insurance.

Dell, Kent P. 2015. "Military and Veterans Affairs." December. http://www.house.mi.gov/hfa/Archives/PDF/MVA_BudgetBriefin g_fy15-16.pdf.

Department of Veterans Affairs Fast Facts. 2016, November 18. http://edition.cnn.com/2014/05/30/us/department-of-veterans-affairs-fast-facts/index.html.

dictionary.com. 2017. s.v. "burden of proof." http://www.dictionary.com/browse/burden-of-proof.

dictionary.com. n.d. s.v. "healthcare." http://www.dictionary.com/browse/health--care.

Douglas-Gabriel, Danielle. 2015. "Students Now Pay More of Their Public Univerisity Tuition than State Governments." January 5. https://www.washingtonpost.com/news/get-there/wp/2015/01/05/students-cover-more-of-their-public-

university-tuition-now-than-state-
governments/?utm_term=.c292007b426d.

Download Your State's Advance Directives. 2005.
http://www.caringinfo.org/i4a/pages/index.cfm?pageid=3289.

Dr. Koop's Abortion Advice. 1989, March 21.
http://www.nytimes.com/1989/03/21/opinion/dr-koop-s-abortion-
advice.html.

Driverless Trucks: A Seismic Shift for the Labor Force. 2017, March 13.
http://www.ttnews.com/articles/basetemplate.aspx?storyid=45239.

Dunbar, John. 2012. "The Citizens United Decision and Why It Matters."
October 18.
https://www.publicintegrity.org/2012/10/18/11527/citizens-
united-decision-and-why-it-matters.

Dunkelberg, William. 2016. "The Hidden Cost of Regulations." July 12.
https://www.forbes.com/sites/williamdunkelberg/2016/07/12/the-
cost-of-regulations/#5f9f7bcb6c81.

Educating the People. 1820.
http://famguardian.org/subjects/politics/thomasjefferson/jeff1350.
htm.

Education at a Glance 2014. 2014. http://dx.doi.org/10.1787/eag-2014-en.

Effective Programs for Stuggling Readers: A Best Evidence Synthesis.
2009, July 7.
http://www.bestevidence.org/word/strug_read_Jul_07_2011_sum.
pdf.

Ekins, Gavin, and Joseph Henchman. 2016. "Marijuana Legalization and
Taxes: Federal Revenue Impact." May 12.
https://taxfoundation.org/marijuana-tax-legalization-federal-
revenue/.

Eligibility. 2017a. https://www.medicaid.gov/medicaid/eligibility/.

Eligibility. 2017b. https://www.medicaid.gov/medicaid-chip-program-information/by-topics/waivers/1115/downloads/list-of-eligibility-groups.pdf.

End-of-Life Care in Canada More Hospital-Centric than in U.S., Europe. 2016, Janurary 19. http://www.cbc.ca/news/health/end-of-life-palliative-hospice-1.3410064.

Enten, Harry. 2016. "American's Distaste for Both Trump and Clinton is Record-Breaking." May 5. https://fivethirtyeight.com/features/americans-distaste-for-both-trump-and-clinton-is-record-breaking/.

Entry-Exit System: Progress, Challenges, and Outlook. 2014, May 6. https://bipartisanpolicy.org/library/immigration-entry-exit-system/.

Escamilla, Javier. n.d. "The Social Security Dilemma." https://web.stanford.edu/class/e297c/poverty_prejudice/soc_sec/hsocialsec.htm.

Exner, Rich. 2016. "How the Age of 2016 Candidates Stack Up to Past US Presidents…" February 1. http://www.cleveland.com/datacentral/index.ssf/2016/02/how_the_age_of_2016_candidates.html.

FAA 2016 Performance & Accountability Report. 2016. https://www.faa.gov/about/plans_reports/media/2016-FAA-PAR.pdf.

Fact-Check: Did 3 Million Undocumented Immigrants Vote in This Year's Election? 2016, November 18. http://www.politifact.com/punditfact/statements/2016/nov/18/blog-posting/no-3-million-undocumented-immigrants-did-not-vote-/.

FAQ about Homeless Veterans. n.d. http://nchv.org/index.php/news/media/background_and_statistics/.

Farah, Stephanie. 2014. "What You Need to Know about Out-of-State Tuition." July 8. http://www.collegexpress.com/interests/public-colleges-and-universities/blog/what-you-need-know-about-out-state-tuition/.

Farber, Madeline. 2017. "Her's How Much President Trump's Wall with Mexico Would Cost." January 25. http://fortune.com/2017/01/25/donald-trump-mexico-wall-cost/.

Fast Facts. 2013. https://nces.ed.gov/fastfacts/display.asp?id=66.

Federal Spending: Where Does the Money Go. 2016. https://www.nationalpriorities.org/budget-basics/federal-budget-101/spending/.

Ferlazzo, Larry. 2016. "Response: How to Practice Restorative Justice in Schools." February 6. http://blogs.edweek.org/teachers/classroom_qa_with_larry_ferlazzo/2016/02/response_how_to_practice_restorative_justice_in_schools.html.

Financial Regulatory Reform: Financial Crisis Losses and Potential Impacts of the Dodd-Frank Act. 2013, February 14. http://www.gao.gov/products/GAO-13-180.

Flores. n.d. "The 1967 Single-Member District Mandate." http://archive.fairvote.org/library/history/flores/district.htm.

45 Percent of Americans Pay No Federal Income Tax. 2016, February 24. http://nypost.com/2016/02/24/45-percent-of-americans-pay-no-federal-income-tax/.

The Foundations of the New Physics. 1900. http://timeline.aps.org/APS/Timeline/?DecadeYear=1900.

Frankel, Todd C. 2015. "New NASA Data Show How the World Is Running Out of Water." June 16. https://www.washingtonpost.com/news/wonk/wp/2015/06/16/new-nasa-studies-show-how-the-world-is-running-out-of-water/?utm_term=.569c4d9f89a7.

Frydman, Carola, and Dirk Jenter. 2010. "CEO Compensation." Rock Center for Corporate Governance at Stanford University Working paper No. 77. https://ssrn.com/abstract=1582232.

Funding/Budget—Annual Report 2015. 2015.
http://www.uscourts.gov/statistics-reports/fundingbudget-annual-report-2015.

Gabler, Neal. 2016. "The Secret Shame of the Middle-Class Americans." May. https://www.theatlantic.com/magazine/archive/2016/05/my-secret-shame/476415/.

GAO High Risk List. 2017.
http://www.gao.gov/highrisk/dod_financial_management/why_did_study.

Gates, Bill. 2017. "Bill Gates Predicts an End to Poverty in 20 Years." March 6. http://www.dailymail.co.uk/news/article-2543302/Bill-Gates-predicts-no-poor-countries-20-years-dispells-myth-foreign-aid-doesnt-work.html.

GDP (Current US$). 2016.
http://data.worldbank.org/indicator/NY.GDP.MKTP.CD.

Gibb, Bruce L. 2016. "DVF>R." Ann Arbor, MI, January.

Gillin, Joshua. 2017. "Newt Gingrich Misleads with Point That House Health Care Bill Grows Medicaid Spending." June 28. http://www.politifact.com/punditfact/statements/2017/jun/28/newt-gingrich/gingrich-misleads-point-house-bill-grows-medicaid-/.

Gleicher, David, Richard Beckhard, and R. Harris. 1987. "Change Formula."
http://www.valuebasedmanagement.net/methods_beckhard_change_model.html.

Goldberg, Michelle. 2014. "Swedish Prostitution Law Is Spreading Worldwide—Here Is How to Improve It." August 8. https://www.theguardian.com/commentisfree/2014/aug/08/criminalise-buying-not-selling-sex.

Goldstein, Joshua S., and Steven Pinker. 2016. "The Decline of War and Violence." April 15.
https://www.bostonglobe.com/opinion/2016/04/15/the-decline-war-and-violence/lxhtEplvppt0Bz9kPphzkL/story.html.

Gomez, Marisa. 2016. "Taxpayers Spent Half a Billion Dollars on Party Primaries in 2016." July 21. https://ivn.us/2016/07/21/taxpayers-spent-half-billion-dollars-on-party-primaries-in-2016/.

Gonzales-Barrera, Ana. 2015. "More Mixicans Leaving than Coming to the U.S." November 19. http://www.pewhispanic.org/2015/11/19/more-mexicans-leaving-than-coming-to-the-u-s/.

Greenspan—I Was Wrong about the Economy. Sort of. 2008, October, Thursday. https://www.theguardian.com/business/2008/oct/24/economics-creditcrunch-federal-reserve-greenspan.

Growth Rate. 2017. http://www.worldometers.info/world-population/.

Gulf War Fast Facts. 2016. August 2. http://www.cnn.com/2013/09/15/world/meast/gulf-war-fast-facts/.

Harrington, Rebecca, and Skye Gould. 2016. "Americans Beat One Voter Turnout Record—Here's How 2016 Compares with Past Elections." December 21. http://www.businessinsider.com/trump-voter-turnout-records-history-obama-clinton-2016-11.

Hart, George W. 1998. "Johannes Kepler's Polyhedra." http://www.georgehart.com/virtual-polyhedra/kepler.html.

HCPCS 2013 Index. 2013. https://www.cms.gov/Medicare/Coding/HCPCSReleaseCodeSets/Downloads/INDEX2013.pdf.

Health Insurance: Premiums and Increases. 2017, January 3. http://www.ncsl.org/research/health/health-insurance-premiums.aspx.

The High Price of Silence: Analyzing the Business Implications of an Under-Vacationed Workforce. 2016, October 12. http://www.projecttimeoff.com/sites/default/files/High_Price-of_Silence_FINAL.pdf.

HIPAA Violations & Enforcement. n.d. https://www.ama-assn.org/practice-management/hipaa-violations-enforcement.

Historical Trends in Federal R&D. 2017. June 2.
https://www.aaas.org/page/historical-trends-federal-rd.

History of Health Insurance Benefits. 2002, March.
https://www.ebri.org/publications/facts/index.cfm?fa=0302fact.

HITECH Act. 2014, December.
http://searchhealthit.techtarget.com/definition/HITECH-Act.

Holan, Angie, and Louis Jacobson. 2011. "Barack Obama Said Social
Security and Other Federal Checks May Not Go Out on Aug. 3 If
the Debt Ceiling Is Not Increased." July 13.
http://www.politifact.com/truth-o-
meter/statements/2011/jul/13/barack-obama/barack-obama-said-
social-security-and-other-federa/.

Howden, Lindsay, and Julie Meyer. 2011. "Age and Sex Composition:
2010." May.
https://www.census.gov/prod/cen2010/briefs/c2010br-03.pdf.

ICD-10 Version:2016. 2016.
http://apps.who.int/classifications/icd10/browse/2016/en.

If You Don't Have Health Insurance: How Much You'll Pay. 2017.
https://www.healthcare.gov/fees/fee-for-not-being-covered/.

Illiteracy Statistics. 2016, August 22.
http://www.statisticbrain.com/number-of-american-adults-who-
cant-read/.

The Impact of Organized Crime in the City of Chicago. n.d.
http://www.umich.edu/~eng217/student_projects/nkazmers/index1
.html.

Impose a 5 Percent Value-Added Tax. 2016, December 8.
https://www.cbo.gov/budget-options/2016/52285.

Index Fund. n.d. http://www.investopedia.com/terms/i/indexfund.asp.

In-State vs. Out-of-State Tuition. 2013. https://www.heath.gwu.edu/state-
vs-out-state-tuition.

Jacobson, Louis. 2015. "Pie Chart of 'Federal Spending' Circulating on
the Internet Is Misleading." August 17.

http://www.politifact.com/truth-o-meter/statements/2015/aug/17/facebook-posts/pie-chart-federal-spending-circulating-internet-mi/.

Jeffrey, Terrence. 2016. "U.S. Has Lost 191,000 Mining Industry Jubs since September 2014." May 6. http://www.cnsnews.com/news/article/terence-p-jeffrey/us-has-lost-191000-mining-jobs-september-2014.

John F. Kennedy Quotes. n.d. http://www.azquotes.com/quote/156204.

Kalmikov, Alex, and Katherine Dykes. n.d. "Wind Power Fundamentals." http://web.mit.edu/windenergy/windweek/Presentations/Wind%20Energy%20101.pdf.

Key Elements of the U.S. Tax System. 2016. http://www.taxpolicycenter.org/briefing-book/how-does-corporate-income-tax-work.

Key Elements of the U.S. Tax System. 2017. http://www.taxpolicycenter.org/briefing-book/what-are-major-federal-payroll-taxes-and-how-much-money-do-they-raise.

Kilmer, Beau, Susan S. Sohler Everingham, Jonathan P. Caulkins, Greg Midgette, Rosalie Liccardo Pacula, Peter H. Reuter, Rachel M. Burns, Bing Han, and Russell Lundberg. 2014. "How Big Is the U.S. Market for Illegal Drugs?" http://www.rand.org/pubs/research_briefs/RB9770.html.

Kim, Victoria, and Frank Shyong. 2017. "'Maternity Tourism' Raids Target California Operations Catering to Chinese." March 6. http://www.latimes.com/local/lanow/la-me-ln-birth-tourism-schemes-raids-20150303-story.html.

Klein, Ezra. 2013. "21 Graphs That Show America's Health-Care Prices Are Ludicrous." March 26. https://www.washingtonpost.com/news/wonk/wp/2013/03/26/21-graphs-that-show-americas-health-care-prices-are-ludicrous/?utm_term=.d83a9efb4e5e.

Kokemuller, Neil. 2016. "How Important Is School Size?" March 4. http://www.greatschools.org/gk/articles/school-size/.

Kolawole, Emi. 2008. "Breakdown of Government Revenue." June 29. http://www.factcheck.org/2008/06/breakdown-of-government-revenue/.

Koop, C. Everett. n.d.a "C. Everett Koop Quotes and Sayings." http://www.inspiringquotes.us/author/9817-c-everett-koop.

———. n.d.b "The C. Everett Koop Papers." https://profiles.nlm.nih.gov/ps/retrieve/Narrative/QQ/p-nid/87.

Laskow, Sarah. 2014. "How Retirement Was Invented." October 24. https://www.theatlantic.com/business/archive/2014/10/how-retirement-was-invented/381802/.

The Latest from PolitiFact. 2017. http://www.politifact.com/.

Lee, Michelle Ye Hee. 2015. "Yes, U.S. Locks People Up at a Higher Rate than Any Other Country." July 7. https://www.washingtonpost.com/news/fact-checker/wp/2015/07/07/yes-u-s-locks-people-up-at-a-higher-rate-than-any-other-country/?utm_term=.8453f618c95d.

Lee, Peter, Scott Regenbogen, and Atul Gawande. 2008. "How Many Surgical Procedures Will Americans Experience in an Average Lifetime? Evidence from Three States." http://www.mcacs.org/abstracts/2008/P15.cgi.

Long, Heather. 2016. "U.S. Inequality Keeps Getting Uglier." December 22. http://money.cnn.com/2016/12/22/news/economy/us-inequality-worse/.

A Look at the Shocking Student Loan Debt Statistics for 2017. 2017, September 13. https://studentloanhero.com/student-loan-debt-statistics/.

Ludington Pumped Storage. 2017. https://www.consumersenergy.com/content.aspx?id=6985.

Luebke, Bob. 2016. "Teacher Pay, Part III: The Rising Cost of Benefits." May 25. https://www.nccivitas.org/2016/18216/.

Lyndon B. Johnson. 1968, February 8.
http://www.presidency.ucsb.edu/ws/?pid=29282.

Madison, James. 1787. "Transcript of Federalist Papers, No. 10 & No. 51 (1787-1788)."
https://www.ourdocuments.gov/doc.php?flash=false&doc=10&page=transcript.

Maginot Line. 2009. http://www.history.com/topics/world-war-ii/maginot-line.

Manhattan Project. 2012. https://www.ctbto.org/nuclear-testing/history-of-nuclear-testing/manhattan-project/.

Margulies, Joseph. 2016. "This Is the Real Reason Private Prisons Should Be Outlawed." August 24. http://time.com/4461791/private-prisons-department-of-justice/.

Martin, Richard. 2015. "China Details Next-gen Nuclear Reactor Program." October 16. https://www.technologyreview.com/s/542526/china-details-next-gen-nuclear-reactor-program/.

Martin, Richard. 2016. "Fail-Safe Nuclear Power." August 2. https://www.technologyreview.com/s/602051/fail-safe-nuclear-power/.

Massachusetts Registered Voter Enrollment: 1948–2016. 2016, October. https://www.sec.state.ma.us/ele/eleenr/enridx.htm.

Matthews, Merrill. 2011. "What Happened to the $2.6 Trillion Social Security Trust Fund?" July 13. https://www.forbes.com/sites/merrillmatthews/2011/07/13/what-happened-to-the-2-6-trillion-social-security-trust-fund/#365b193f4947.

McCaherty, Joshua. 2014. "The Cost of Tax Compliance." September 11. https://taxfoundation.org/cost-tax-compliance/.

Mckenzie, Joi-Marie. 2017. "High School Senior Creates Group 'We Dine Together' so No Student Has to Eat Alone." March 16.

http://abcnews.go.com/Lifestyle/high-school-senior-creates-group-dine-student-eat/story?id=46172969.

Medicare Part B Costs. 2017. https://www.medicareinteractive.org/get-answers/how-original-medicare-works/original-medicare-cost-overview/medicare-part-b-costs.

Members of Congress. 2017. https://www.govtrack.us/congress/members.

Merriam-Webster OnLine. n.d. s.v. "conservative." https://www.merriam-webster.com/dictionary/conservative.

Merritt, Cam. 2010. "What Percent of IRS Revenue Comes from Capital Gains Tax?" http://thefinancebase.com/percent-irs-revenue-comes-capital-gains-tax-1105.html.

Michaels, Dave. 2009. "On NextGen, Everything Is Clear except Who Pays for It." March. https://www.dallasnews.com/business/airlines/2009/03/30/on-nextgen-everything-clear-ex.

Military Education. 2003. http://www.gao.gov/new.items/d031000.pdf.

Misquoting Ymamoto. 2009, May 11. http://www.factcheck.org/2009/05/misquoting-yamamoto/.

Mohney, Gillian. 2016. "The Remarkable Cancer Treatment That Helped Jimmy Carter Combat Brain Tumor." March 7. http://abcnews.go.com/Health/remarkable-cancer-treatment-helped-jimmy-carter-combat-brain/story?id=37467459.

Moody's $864m Penalty for Ratings in Run-up to 2008 Financial Crisis. 2017, January 14. https://www.theguardian.com/business/2017/jan/14/moodys-864m-penalty-for-ratings-in-run-up-to-2008-financial-crisis.

More Workers Enroll in High Deductible Plans…2016, September 14. http://www.kff.org/health-costs/press-release/average-annual-workplace-family-health-premiums-rise-modest-3-to-18142-in-2016-more-workers-enroll-in-high-deductible-plans-with-savings-option-over-past-two-years/.

Morgenson, Gretchen. 2016. "Portland Adopts Surcharge on C.E.O. Pay in Move vs. Income Inequality." December 7.

https://www.nytimes.com/2016/12/07/business/economy/portland
-oregon-tax-executive-pay.html.

Mufson, Steven. 2015. "Obama's Proposal to Raise the Capital Gains Tax
Drives Sharp Wedge between Parties." January 20.
https://www.washingtonpost.com/business/economy/obamas-
proposal-to-raise-the-capital-gains-tax-drives-sharp-wedge-
between-parties/2015/01/20/85eafb64-a0c1-11e4-903f-
9f2faf7cd9fe_story.html?utm_term=.3a532e170533.

Mulhere, Kaitlin. 2017. "Trump's Budget Would Kill the Beloved
Volunteer Program AmeriCorps." March 16.
http://time.com/money/4703924/trump-budget-americorps-
college-funding-cut/.

Nagourney, Adam. 2012. "California Set to Send Many New faces to
Washington." *New York Times*, February 13.
http://www.nytimes.com/2012/02/14/us/california-congressional-
delegation-braces-for-change.html.

Nargund, G. 2009. "Declining Birth Rate in Developed Countries: A
Radical Policy Re-think Is Required."
https://www.ncbi.nlm.nih.gov/pmc/articles/PMC4255510/.

Nation's Schools Facing Largest Teacher Retirement Wave in History.
2011, June 24. https://nctaf.org/announcements/nations-schools-
facing-largest-teacher-retirement-wave-in-history/.

Nationwide Trends. 2015, June.
https://www.drugabuse.gov/publications/drugfacts/nationwide-
trends.

New Device Makes Wheelchairs Obsolete. 2012, March 23.
https://www.youtube.com/watch?v=VE-l7uH91jM.

New York Times. 1993. "Birth Control 'for All People.'" April 2.
Accessed February 21, 2011.
http://query.nytimes.com/gst/fullpage.html?res=9F0CE1DA1239F
931A35757C0A965958260.

Newcomb, Alyssa. 2016. "Intel CEO Says Reports of the Death of Moore's Law Have Been Greatly Exaggerated." April 27. http://abcnews.go.com/Technology/intel-ceo-reports-death-moores-law-greatly-exaggerated/story?id=38703042.

Nieto, Enrique Pena. 2017. "Trump: To Get Started, Mexico Will Pay for the Wall." January 11. http://www.politico.com/story/2017/01/trump-presser-mexico-border-wall-233482.

Non-Driver State ID. n.d. http://www.nyc.gov/html/id/html/how/state_id.shtml.

Norman, Jim. 2017. "Congress Approval Drops to 20% after February High." April. http://www.gallup.com/poll/208472/congress-approval-drops-down-february-high.aspx.

Nowrasteh, Alex. 2010. "5 Reasons Why America Should Steer Clear of a National ID Card." March 9. http://www.foxnews.com/opinion/2010/03/09/alex-nowrasteh-national-id-e-verify-illegal-immigration.html.

O'Donnell, Norah. 2016. "Are Members of Congress Becoming Telemarketers?" April 24. http://www.cbsnews.com/news/60-minutes-are-members-of-congress-becoming-telemarketers/.

The Office of Audit. n.d. http://oig.ssa.gov/about-oig/offices/office-audit.

Options for Reducing the Deficit: 2014 to 2023. 2013, November 13. https://www.cbo.gov/budget-options/2013/44854.

Organizing and Staffing. n.d. https://www.cbo.gov/about/organization-and-staffing.

Osborn, Robin, and Cathy Schoen. 2013. "The Commonwealth Fund 2013 International Health Policy Survey in Eleven Countries." November. http://www.commonwealthfund.org/~/media/files/publications/in-the-literature/2013/nov/pdf_schoen_2013_ihp_survey_chartpack_final.pdf.

Otto von Bismarck. n.d. https://www.ssa.gov/history/ottob.html.

Paltrow, Scot J. 2016. "U.S. Army Fudged Its Accounts by Trillions of Dollars, Auditor Finds." August 19. http://www.reuters.com/article/us-usa-audit-army-idUSKCN10U1IG.

Parker, Tim. 2016. "The Average Retirement Savings by Age for 2016." December 8. http://www.investopedia.com/articles/personal-finance/011216/average-retirement-savings-age-2016.asp.

Passell, Peter, and Leonard Ross. 1973. "Daniel Moynihan and President-elect Nixon: How Charity Didn't Begin at Home." January 14. http://www.nytimes.com/books/98/10/04/specials/moynihan-income.html.

Phonics Basics. 2017. http://www.pbs.org/parents/education/reading-language/reading-tips/phonics-basics/.

Plumer, Brad. 2017. "U.S. Nuclear Comeback Stalls as Two Reactors Are Abandoned." July 31. https://www.nytimes.com/2017/07/31/climate/nuclear-power-project-canceled-in-south-carolina.html.

Pomerleau, Kyle, and Emily Potosky. 2016. "Corporate Income Tax Rates around the World, 2016." August 18. https://taxfoundation.org/corporate-income-tax-rates-around-world-2016/.

Priori, Silvia. 2014. "Genetic Testing to Predict Sudden Cardiac Death: Current Perspectives and Future Goals." January. https://www.ncbi.nlm.nih.gov/pmc/articles/PMC4237297/.

Pumped-Storage Hydro Plants. n.d. https://www.duke-energy.com/energy-education/how-energy-works/pumped-storage-hydro-plants.

Pyper, Julia. 2016. "Michigan Passes Legislation to Boost Renewables Mandate, Retain Net Metering." December 16. https://www.greentechmedia.com/articles/read/michigan-passes-bills-to-boost-renewables-mandate-retain-net-metering.

Ramsey, Lydia. 2017. "The Cost of an MRI Can Vary by Thousands of Dollars Depending on Where You Go." March 28.

http://uk.businessinsider.com/how-much-an-mri-costs-by-state-2017-3?r=US&IR=T.

Ranked Choice Voting. 2017. http://www.fairvote.org/.

Raskin, Jamie. 2014. "A Shareholder Solution to 'Citizens United.'" October 3. https://www.washingtonpost.com/opinions/a-shareholder-solution-to-citizens-united/2014/10/03/5e07c3ee-48be-11e4-b72e-d60a9229cc10_story.html?utm_term=.656167ac01de.

Reay, Rebecca, Milla Sanes, and John Schmitt. 2013. "No-Vacation Nation Revisited." May. http://cepr.net/publications/reports/no-vacation-nation-2013.

Regalado, Antonio. 2015. "Biotech's Coming Cancer Cure." June 18. https://www.technologyreview.com/s/538441/biotechs-coming-cancer-cure/.

Reilly, Michael. 2012. "AI Predicts When You're about to Get Sick." July 26. https://www.newscientist.com/blogs/onepercent/2012/07/ai-predicts-when-youre-about-t.html.

Report on the Economic Well-Being of U.S. Households in 2014. 2014. https://www.federalreserve.gov/econresdata/2015-economic-well-being-of-us-households-in-2014-executive-summary.htm.

Report: U.S. Global Lead in R&D at Risk as China Rises. 2016, February. https://www.aip.org/fyi/2016/report-us-global-lead-rd-risk-china-rises.

Reston, Laura. 2017. "Russia Has Weaponized Fake News to Sow Chaos." May 12. https://newrepublic.com/article/142344/russia-weaponized-fake-news-sow-chaos.

Rincon, Paul. 2014. "Richard II's DNA Throws Up Infidelity Surprise." December 2. http://www.bbc.com/news/science-environment-30281333.

Robinson, Kenneth. n.d. "Savings and Loan Crisis." http://www.federalreservehistory.org/Events/DetailView/42.

Rovner, Julie. 2016. "A Record Percentage of Americans Now Have Health Insurance." September 13.

http://time.com/money/4490196/health-insurance-coverage-census-2015/.

Sahadi, Jeanne. 2016. "It's Good to Be a Working Parent in Europe." February 19. http://money.cnn.com/2016/02/17/pf/working-parents-paid-leave/.

Sanders, Katie. 2015. "Stephen Colbert Brings Up Ronald Reagan's Tax-Raising Record in Ted Cruz Interview." September 25. http://www.politifact.com/punditfact/statements/2015/sep/25/stephen-colbert/stephen-colbert-brings-ronald-reagans-tax-raising-/.

Santora, Marc. 2013. "City's Annual Cost per Inmate Is $168,000." August 23. https://mobile.nytimes.com/2013/08/24/nyregion/citys-annual-cost-per-inmate-is-nearly-168000-study-says.html.

Saplakoglu, Yasemin. 2017. "New Gene Drive Technology Could Wipe Out Malaria, but Is It Safe?" February 19. http://www.sciencemag.org/news/2017/02/new-gene-drive-technology-could-wipe-out-malaria-it-safe.

Schedule of Federal Debt. 2014, December 31. https://www.treasurydirect.gov/govt/reports/pd/feddebt/feddebt_dec14.pdf.

Schools and Staffing Survey. 2009. https://nces.ed.gov/surveys/sass/tables/sass0708_035_s1s.asp.

Sea Level Rise. 2017. http://www.climatecentral.org/what-we-do/our-programs/sea-level-rise.

Selby, W. Gardner. 2015. "Jeremy Bird Says 90 percent of Americans Want Mandatory Background Checks for All Gun Purchases." October 5. http://www.politifact.com/texas/statements/2015/oct/05/jeremy-bird/jeremy-bird-says-90-percent-americans-want-mandato/.

Select Grammar and Writing Style Options in Office 2016. 2016. https://support.office.com/en-us/article/Select-grammar-and-writing-style-options-in-Office-2016-ecd60e9f-6b2e-4070-b30c-42efa6cff55a.

Serbu, Jared. 2017. "As Key Deadline Approaches, DoD Remains Biggest Obstacle to Governmentwide Audit." January 24. https://federalnewsradio.com/dod-reporters-notebook-jared-serbu/2017/01/key-deadline-approaches-dod-remains-biggest-obstacle-governmentwide-audit/.

Sharpe, Susan. 1998. "A Restorative Justice Agency." http://www.insightprisonproject.org/a-restorative-justice-agency.html.

Sinskey, Christine, Lacey Colligan, Ling Li, MIrela Prgomet, Sam Reynolds, Lindsey Goeders, Johanna Westbrook, Michael Tutty, and George Blike. 2016. "Allocation of Physician Time in Ambulatory Practice: A Time and Motion Study in 4 Specialties." December 6. http://annals.org/aim/article/2546704/allocation-physician-time-ambulatory-practice-time-motion-study-4-specialties.

Sixteenth Amendment. n.d. http://legal-dictionary.thefreedictionary.com/sixteenth+amendment.

Smith, Joy M. P. 2014. "Our New Prostitution Bill Protects the Dignity of Women and Youth." June 6. http://www.huffingtonpost.ca/joy-smith-mp/prostitution-bill-canada_b_5459921.html.

Sodha, Sonia. 2017. "Is Findland's Basic Universal Income a Solution to Automation, Fewer Jobs and Lower Wages?" February 19. https://www.theguardian.com/society/2017/feb/19/basic-income-finland-low-wages-fewer-jobs.

Solar Roof. 2017. https://www.tesla.com/solar.

Sorensen, Kirk Frederick. 2014. "Thorium Research in the Manhattan Project Era." May. https://www.scribd.com/document/284613442/Thorium-Research-in-the-Manhattan-Project-Era-Kirk-Sorensen-pdf.

Spear, Andrew. 2016. "Here's How IBM Watson Health Is Transforming the Health Care Industry." April 5. http://fortune.com/ibm-watson-health-business-strategy/.

Spiller, Beia. 2015. "All Electricity Is Not Priced Equally: Time-Variant Pricing 101." January 27. http://blogs.edf.org/energyexchange/2015/01/27/all-electricity-is-not-priced-equally-time-variant-pricing-101/.

Starr, Bernard. 2017. "On the Verge of Immortality, or Are We Stuck with Death? A New Direction for Research Could Provide the Answers—and More." January 14. http://www.huffingtonpost.com/bernard-starr/on-the-verge-of-immortali_b_14133856.html.

States with Initiative or Referendum. 2017. https://ballotpedia.org/States_with_initiative_or_referendum.

Status Report of the U.S. Government Gold Reserve. 2017, February 28. https://www.fiscal.treasury.gov/fsreports/rpt/goldRpt/current_report.htm.

Stewart, Scott. 2013. "Mexico's Cartels and the Economics of Cocaine." January 3. https://www.stratfor.com/weekly/mexicos-cartels-and-economics-cocaine.

Straubel, J. B. 2014. "Driving Range for the Model S Family." https://www.tesla.com/fi_FI/blog/driving-range-model-s-family.

Strauss, Valerie. 2012. "Survey: Teachers Work 53 Hours per Week on Average." March 16. https://www.washingtonpost.com/blogs/answer-sheet/post/survey-teachers-work-53-hours-per-week-on-average/2012/03/16/gIQAqGxYGS_blog.html?utm_term=.0bb3f6bc890c.

Stringer, Scott M. 2015. "The Hardest Working Cities." March. http://comptroller.nyc.gov/wp-content/uploads/documents/Longest_Work_Weeks_March_2015.pdf.

A Summary of the 2016 Annual Reports. 2016. https://www.ssa.gov/oact/trsum/.

Superfund. 2017, March 1. https://www.epa.gov/Superfund.

Supporting the Human Right to Death with Dignity. 2017.
http://www.finalexitnetwork.org/.

Tasselmyer, Michael. 2015. "A Complex Problem: The Compliance
Burdens of the Tax Code." April 8.
http://www.ntu.org/foundation/policy-paper/a-complex-problem-
the-compliance-burdens-of-the-tax-code.

Taylor, Adam, and Laris Karklis. 2016. "This Remarkable Chart Shows
How U.S. Defense Spending Dwarfs the Rest of the World."
February 9.
https://www.washingtonpost.com/news/worldviews/wp/2016/02/0
9/this-remarkable-chart-shows-how-u-s-defense-spending-dwarfs-
the-rest-of-the-world/?utm_term=.fc09cdb5a845.

Thomson Reuters Westlaw. n.d.
http://legalsolutions.thomsonreuters.com/law-products/westlaw-
legal-research/.

Time. 1959. "POLITICS: The Birth Control Issue." December 7.
Accessed February 21, 2011.
http://www.time.com/time/magazine/article/0,9171,811501-
2,00.html.

Topic 701—Sale of Your Home. 2017, April 15.
https://www.irs.gov/taxtopics/tc701.html.

Toyota iBOT Wheelchair. 2016, May 23.
https://www.youtube.com/watch?v=9qYz2wsVKYE.

Tretkoff, Ernie. 2017. "Discovery of Nuclear Fission."
https://www.aps.org/publications/apsnews/200712/physicshistory.
cfm.

Trump, Donald. 2015. "I'll Build a Wall and Mexico Will Pay for It."
June 15. http://insider.foxnews.com/2015/06/16/watch-highlights-
donald-trumps-2016-announcement-ill-build-border-wall-and-
mexico-will.

———. 2017. "Trump: To Get Started, Mexico Will Pay for the Wall."
January 11. http://www.politico.com/story/2017/01/trump-presser-
mexico-border-wall-233482.

Trust Fund. n.d. http://www.investopedia.com/terms/t/trust-fund.asp.

Tsang, Derek. 2014. "Does the U.S. Have the Highest Corporate Tax Rate in the Free World?" September 9. http://www.politifact.com/punditfact/statements/2014/sep/09/eric-bolling/does-us-have-highest-corporate-tax-rate-free-world/.

Tuition Costs of Colleges and Universities. 2014. https://nces.ed.gov/fastfacts/display.asp?id=76.

Turning Back the Aging Clock. 2016. November 18. http://www.caltech.edu/news/turning-back-aging-clock-53030.

2005 Kashmir Earthquake. 2009. http://www.history.com/topics/kashmir-earthquake.

2013 Chevrolet Volt for Sale. 2017, July 4. https://www.autotrader.com/cars-for-sale/2013/Chevrolet/Volt/Chelsea+MI-48118?zip=48118&startYear=2013&numRecords=25&sortBy=derivedpriceDESC&firstRecord=0&endYear=2013&modelCodeList=VOLT&makeCodeList=CHEV&searchRadius=0.

2017 United States Budget Estimate. 2017. http://federal-budget.insidegov.com/l/120/2017-Estimate.

Upbin, Bruce. 2013. "Learn to Read Chinese in Eight Minutes." April 25. https://www.forbes.com/sites/bruceupbin/2013/04/25/learn-to-read-chinese-in-eight-minutes/#49220b701795.

U.S. and World Population Clock. 2017. February 12. http://www.census.gov/popclock/.

US Bureau of Economic Analysis. 2016. "Shares of Gross Domestic Income." August 5. https://fred.stlouisfed.org/series/W270RE1A156NBEA.

U.S. Citizenship. 2013. January 17. https://www.uscis.gov/us-citizenship.

US R&D Spending at an All-Time High, Federal Share Reaches Record Low. 2016, November. https://www.aip.org/fyi/2016/us-rd-spending-all-time-high-federal-share-reaches-record-low.

US Securities and Exchange Commission. 2015. "U.S. Securities and Exchange Commission." August 5. https://www.sec.gov/news/pressrelease/2015-160.html.

VanZant, Kevin. n.d. "The Land Ordinance of 1785 and the Northwest Ordinance of 1787." https://www3.nd.edu/~rbarger/www7/ord17857.html.

Vedantam, Shankar. 2013. "When Crime Pays: Prison Can Teach Some to Be Better Criminals." February 1. http://www.npr.org/2013/02/01/169732840/when-crime-pays-prison-can-teach-some-to-be-better-criminals.

Vikram. n.d. "Get Your Facts Right—6 Fact Checking Websites That Help You Know the Truth." https://www.technorms.com/454/get-your-facts-right-6-fact-checking-websites-that-help-you-know-the-truth.

Vince, Gaia. 2012. "How the World's Oceans Could Be Running Out of Fish." September 21. http://www.bbc.com/future/story/20120920-are-we-running-out-of-fish.

Viswanatha, Aruna, and Karen Freifeld. 2015. "S&P Reaches $1.5 Billion Deal with U.S., States over Crisis-Era Ratings." February 3. http://www.reuters.com/article/us-s-p-settlement-idUSKBN0L71C120150203.

Volunteer. 2017. http://readingpartners.org/volunteer/.

Wagner, Peter, and Bernadette Rabuy. 2016. "Mass Incarceration: The Whole Pie 2016." March 14. https://www.prisonpolicy.org/reports/pie2016.html.

Weisman, Steven R. 2010. *Daniel Patrick Moynihan: A Portrait in Letters of an American Visionary*. Moynihan Estate.

Westcott, Ben. 2017. "Trump Praises Australia's Universal Health Care after Obamacare Repeal." May 5. http://www.cnn.com/2017/05/04/politics/trump-us-australia-health-care/index.html.

What Do I Have to Pay for Services Covered Under Medicare Part A? 2017. https://www.medicareinteractive.org/get-answers/how-original-medicare-works/original-medicare-cost-overview/what-do-i-have-to-pay-for-services-covered-under-medicare-part-a.

What Does Medicare Cover (Parts A, B, C, and D)? 2017.
https://www.medicareinteractive.org/get-answers/introduction-to-medicare/explaining-medicare/what-does-medicare-cover-parts-a-b-c-and-d.

What Is the Definition of a Reliable Source? 2017.
https://www.reference.com/education/definition-reliable-source-e8c87b325117b2f5#.

Who Are the Remaining Uninsured Americans? 2017.
http://www.healthedeals.com/articles/who-are-the-remaining-uninsured-americans.

WikiHow to Get Involved in Local Politics. n.d.
http://www.wikihow.com/Get-Involved-in-Local-Politics.

Williams, Roberton. 2015. "New Estimates of How Many Households Pay No Federal Income Tax." October 6.
https://www.forbes.com/sites/beltway/2015/10/06/new-estimates-of-how-many-households-pay-no-federal-income-tax/#25757a7261cb.

Williamson, Owen M. 2017. "Master List of Logical Fallacies." February.
http://utminers.utep.edu/omwilliamson/ENGL1311/fallacies.htm.

Winstock, Adam, Monica Barratt, Jason Ferris, and Larissa Maier. 2017. "Global Drug Survey 2017."
https://www.globaldrugsurvey.com/wp-content/themes/globaldrugsurvey/results/GDS2017_key-findings-report_final.pdf.

Wolff, Nancy, Cynthia L. Blitz, Jing Shi, Ronet Bachman, and Jane A. Siegel. 2006. "Sexual Violence inside Prisons: Rates of Victimization." May 23.
https://www.ncbi.nlm.nih.gov/pmc/articles/PMC2438589/.

Woody, Christopher. 2016. "NARCONOMICS: 'The Real Drug
     Millionaires Are Right Here in the United States.'" March 16.
     http://www.businessinsider.com/where-drug-money-goes-2016-3.

World Population Projected to Reach 9.7 Billion by 2050. 2015, July 29.
     http://www.un.org/en/development/desa/news/population/2015-
     report.html.

Young, Jeffrey, and Chris Kirkham. 2013. "Hospital Prices No Longer
     Secret as New Data Reveals Bewildering System, Staggering Cost
     Differences." May 8.
     http://www.huffingtonpost.com/2013/05/08/hospital-prices-cost-
     differences_n_3232678.html.